MORE
THAN
A TICKET TO HEAVEN

*101 days discovering your identity,
inheritance, and influence as a
child of God.*

To Becky,
May the Holy Spirit
reveal more of His,
power in you!
Wendy Lee Kremer

Wendy Lee Kremer

ISBN 978-1-63874-389-7 (paperback)
ISBN 978-1-68570-388-2 (hardcover)
ISBN 978-1-63874-390-3 (digital)

Christian Faith Publishing
832 Park Avenue
Meadville, PA 16335
www.christianfaithpublishing.com

Printed in the United States of America

Praise for "More Than a Ticket to Heaven"

Most believers choose to keep God at a safe and comfortable distance. In what they call "the fear of God," they regard Him respectfully, theologically, religiously—anything but intimately, which can seem a bit scary to them. In her devotional, *More Than a Ticket to Heaven*, Wendy Lee Kremer invites the reader to explore more deeply their rights and privileges as children of God. Her devotionals coax you forward into a richer, deeper, more satisfying walk with your Maker, confident that He holds your very best life in a loving embrace, waiting just for you.

—Stephen Bransford, executive producer
Andrew Wommack Television
Author, "*You've Got a Story; and it's better than you think.*"
Stephenbransford.com

I read this book during one of the toughest times in my life, and it was life-giving! This daily devotional will help you renew your mind and consequently change your life. It will teach you and remind you of God's promises for you as His son or daughter. No matter the page you read, it will be powerful and revealing. You will surely know that your Heavenly Father is speaking to you, the message you need for that very day.

—Benjamin Diaz, senior pastor
Vida Church, Mesa, Arizona

This book is an absolute blessing and a gift to me! With the turn of each page, I felt God's presence in the beautiful heartfelt messages which give clarity to the daily scriptures. Wendy's writing makes the Word of God come alive, teaching us how to apply the truths to our daily lives. Each daily devotional will remind you of God's love, filling your heart, opening your mind, refreshing your soul, and encouraging you to trust God more. The prayer at the end of each daily message will give you the peace, comfort, and strength to prepare you for the day ahead. *More Than a Ticket to Heaven* is a blessing that could not have come at a better time in our lives.

—Cindy Osbrink, Hollywood talent agent
The Osbrink Agency, Burbank, California

Reading *More Than a Ticket to Heaven* has challenged me, motivated me, and at times forced me to look outside of myself and reach out to the people that God has put in my life. It is a wonderful devotional and a great way to start your day. I love this book because every day, the Word of God gets inside of you and empowers you to handle whatever this world tries to throw at you.

—Jim McKimmy, entrepreneur/businessman

Wendy and I have been friends for almost twenty years, and in that time, I've watched her grow in the truth of who she is in Christ. Her understanding of our identity in Christ became so clear; she was compelled to share her understanding through her blog and internet postings so that others could know this truth which sets us all free. After years of posting what God has shown her, I encouraged her to put these postings in a devotional book to bless others with these truths. All of us need a daily reminder of how much God loves us and who we are as a child of the king of the universe. This devotional has the truths and scriptures God has laid on Wendy's heart, and they will greatly bless you.

—Kathleen Jackson, founder
Abound in Hope International

I invite you to read *More than a Ticket to Heaven*. Wendy Lee Kremer never fails to touch my heart with her daily devotions. Her messages will enrich your life, remind you of God's love and forgiveness, and help you keep a clear perspective of eternal life. I was able to get through a huge tough patch in my life with her daily scriptures and lessons from God's Word. I am forever grateful for her book. I believe everyone who reads this book will be blessed as I've been. It will remind you to never give up on the promises of God.

—John Lee Hoich, entrepreneur/philanthropist
Author, *From the Ground Up*

To my parents,
First Lt. Peter A. MacBurnie and Gwendolyn MacBurnie Honeywell
Although you are enjoying life in heaven with Jesus now, what you
sowed into my life here on earth continues to produce a harvest for the
kingdom of God. Your godly examples have instilled in me a passion
for the Word of God and unwavering belief in His faithfulness.
You've left me a priceless legacy!

To my loving husband, Don, and my precious family.
My constant prayer is that you fully experience the height,
depth, width, and breadth of God's unconditional, off-the-
charts love for you and that you fulfill God's unique plan
and destiny for your life. I love you with all my heart!

To my dear friend
Kathy Jackson
My Barnabas encourager!
Without you, this book would not exist. Thank you for
believing in me, praying for me and motivating me to keep
writing. You are a perfect example of a faithful friend.

The heartfelt counsel of a faithful friend is
as sweet as perfume and incense

—Proverbs 27:9, NLT

Introduction

I grew up attending a mainstream denominational church. If there was a service, we were there. Sunday morning, Sunday evening, Wednesday evening, special meetings—we never missed. We were easy to find—the second row from the front on the left side.

I learned a lot of Bible facts, Old Testament stories, and lots of laws. I excelled at Bible trivia and sword drills. I knew that Jesus died on the cross and rose again. I accepted Him as my Savior and was baptized on Easter Sunday when I was thirteen. Reflecting on those days, I learned all the dos and don'ts, but I had no power to do the dos. As I reached high school, I found that being a Christian was cutting into my social life. It appeared that the world had a lot more fun to offer than the Christian life. So I did what a lot of kids did—I rebelled.

It wasn't until I had a very near-death experience in my thirties that God, who never let me stray too far, lovingly drew me back to Himself. As I was recovering from a brain tumor that almost took my life, the one thought that haunted me and finally brought me back to God was...

What if I had died?

I couldn't say for sure that I would spend eternity in heaven.

I don't believe that God ever brings tragedy on us, but looking back on it, I thank Him that he used what the enemy meant to destroy me and made it the turning point of my life.

I was a divorced single mom with two children when I started on my quest to get to know the God who had given me a second chance. I wanted to grasp the truth about God and His love and grace. I knew there had to be more to the Christian life than what I had experienced in my youth. I remarried; and my husband, Don, who grew up as a Mennonite, joined me on this search for the truth and the power behind it. Over the years, we made it our aim to know the true God of the Bible—the God of miracles, the God of grace and mercy rather than a legalistic interpretation. It was exciting to grow in the revelation of the inheritance and the victory Jesus won for us through His resurrection.

Over the years, as I've studied the Word of God, I have grown in my hatred for religion. Did you know that Jesus hated religion? Think about it: the only people to whom Jesus showed disdain and disgust were the religious leaders. He called them a "brood of vipers" and "white-washed tombs." I realized that religion is man's attempt to get to God through works. True Christianity is trusting that Jesus did it all for us. We must simply accept His gift. It's through grace that we are saved by faith.

Lies exposed

I started praying that God would uproot from my heart all the lies. I prayed that every false religious teaching that I had learned growing up with would be exposed and that only the actual truth of God's Word would remain. No one meant to lie to me; it was just traditions of men, teaching from church leaders passed down through the generations that we accepted as truth but without scriptural basis.

As I grew in my passion for knowing God and digging into the Word of God every day, I asked the Holy Spirit, my mentor, to "show me wonderful things from God's Word." He has been faithful to answer me. I have written journals full of these beautiful truths, powerful promises, and applicable insights for life and business—many that I am excited to share with you in this book!

Favor and blessings manifested

My husband and I have used these biblical principles in business—first in building a successful trucking company and then creating an award-winning online nutrition business that has impacted countless families internationally. I have had the privilege of speaking to thousands; preaching at church services; and training business leaders in many countries, from the U.S. to South Africa, Europe, Germany, Ecuador, Malta, Mexico, and more.

I believe that to indeed be successful in family, life, and business, you need a transforming revelation of God's love and grace and His desire for an intimate relationship with you.

I pray that as you read this book and meditate on the truths of your blood-bought identity, inheritance, and influence as a child of God, that you will gain insights that will impact every area of your life and build the kingdom of God!

Are You a Child of God?

I am so glad you've picked up my book today! You're about to read some valuable promises and truths that are absolutely true for every child of God. So first, it's important to answer this question: Are you a child of God?

Everyone is welcome to join God's family. It's strictly your choice. Jesus made you acceptable to Father God through His sacrifice on the cross. He died and rose again so that you could be set free from the penalty of sin and become a member of God's family—His child.

You may have grown up in church, but to join the family of God, you must personally tell the Father that you accept Jesus' gift of salvation and be born-again.

> *But as many as received Him, to them He gave the right to become children of God, to those who believe in His name. (John 1:12)*

Jesus is the only way to heaven.

> *Jesus said to him, "I am the way, the truth, and the life. No one comes to the Father except through Me." (John 14:6)*

The formula to receive from God is to believe and speak:

> *If you confess with your mouth the Lord Jesus and believe in your heart that God has raised Him from the dead, you will be saved. For with the heart one believes*

unto righteousness, and with the mouth confession is made unto salvation. (Romans 10:9–10)

Here's a sample prayer to receive Jesus' gift of salvation and become a child of God:

Jesus, I believe and confess that You are my Lord and Savior. Thank You, Jesus, for dying in my place, and I believe that God raised You back to life. Thank You for taking my sins and making me acceptable to God. Today I am born again to a new life in Jesus Christ. By faith in Your Word I receive salvation now. Amen!

Please send me a message and let me know if you prayed this prayer for the first time. Email me at wendy@wendyleekremer.com, I would love to hear from you!

Day 1

CHILD OF GOD WITH
POWER OF ATTORNEY

I tell you the truth, you will ask the Father directly, and
he will grant your request because you use my name.
You haven't done this before. Ask, using my name, and
you will receive, and you will have abundant joy.

—John 16:23–24

From the beginning of Genesis until Jesus' humble arrival on earth's stage, sinful man required a mediator to approach God; Levitical priests offered continuous sacrifices on behalf of the people.

However, when Jesus became our mediator, everything changed. He not only was pure and holy Himself but through His sacrifice on the cross, Jesus actually cleansed and purified us once for all.

With His blood, He made us righteous and acceptable to God. And more than that, Jesus told his followers, "Use my name when you talk to the Father." This was a radical directive to the disciples. In legal terms, Jesus was granting them power of attorney.

When my mother was advanced in age and needed help with her finances, she gave me power of attorney. With this legal document, I could sell her house, purchase or sell her stock, and act on her behalf in all legal matters. When bankers or the court saw that I held power of attorney, they followed my instructions as if my mother spoke to them directly.

Jesus has given you power of attorney here on earth. When you pray "in the name of Jesus," with faith and belief in your heart, God grants your request the same as if Jesus was personally making the petition. So you can expect the same faithful and generous response from the Father that Jesus would get!

When you pray "in Jesus' name," it is Jesus' worthiness that God evaluates, not yours. So come to the Father boldly, expectantly, and confident that you will get a *yes* answer every time you pray God's Word.

If you doubt that God will answer your prayer when you pray in Jesus' name, the Bible refers to that as *"using the Lord's name in vain"* (Deuteronomy 5:11). Don't do that!

I hope you will meditate on our verse for today. Jesus is instructing you, a child of God, to ask the Father, using his name, *and receive*. What is it you need today? A relationship restored? Provision? Protection? Use the legal authority Jesus granted you to ask and receive what you need so that you will have abundant joy!

A PRAYER FOR TODAY

Father, I come to You today in the name of Jesus and ask that as I read this book, I will gain a deeper revelation of my identity as Your child and the inheritance that Jesus bought for me through His blood. I pray that I'll also realize the positive influence I can have in this world through Your Holy Spirit.

Day 2

CHILD OF GOD DESTINED FOR GREAT EXPLOITS

*Those who do wickedly against the covenant he shall
corrupt with flattery; but the people who know their
God shall be strong, and carry out great exploits.*

—Daniel 11:32

Many people raise their eyebrows and get a puzzled look on their face when I tell them at age sixty-five, I graduated from Charis Bible College. They ask me, "Why? Are you going to be a preacher?"

The last half of Daniel 11:32 holds the answer. I want to do great exploits for God. Do you? Our world is desperate for God's kids—of all ages—to demonstrate the power of God.

To accomplish breathtaking, record-breaking supernatural exploits, we must know our awesome God, have a revelation of His power working in us, and seize hold of His covenant promises. With that knowledge, we will carry out great exploits!

Daniel was a man who knew God. When King Darius issued a decree prohibiting people from praying to any god except the king or be cast into the lion's den, Daniel went right on praying to the God of heaven (Daniel 6:4–15) in front of an open window! Not even the threat of death could keep him from it. He knew his God, and people who know God have the courage and strength to do His will, even though the whole world seems to be against them.

In Daniel chapter 3, we read about Shadrach, Meshach, and Abednego who also knew their God. They refused to worship the golden image and were thrown into the fiery furnace. They knew their all-powerful God who was able to deliver them. They believed He would. And He did!

The Lord is looking for ordinary believers through whom He can display His extraordinary power and grace. He wants to do mighty deeds on the earth but needs willing children of God to work through. God is raising up a people who will know Him intimately, who will be transformed into His image, seize hold of His promises, and do great exploits.

Will you step up to the challenge? God isn't impressed by what you can do on your own; He wants to do great exploits through your life that only *He* can do, the kind where people say, "That *had* to be God!"

A Prayer for Today

Dear God of miracles, sign me up for Your power team! Transform me with knowledge of You. I want to be Your hands and feet and mouthpiece to do the impossible in Your kingdom and make You famous on earth today!

Day 3

WORD-EMPOWERED CHILD OF GOD

If you confess with your mouth the Lord Jesus and believe in your heart that God has raised Him from the dead, you will be saved. For with the heart one believes unto righteousness, and with the mouth confession is made unto salvation.

—Romans 10:9–10

I overheard an adorable curlyhead blond three-year-old little girl talking to her mother in a store recently. She put her hands on her hips and said, "Seriously, Mom? That's not cool!" Now where do you think she picked up that lingo?

We adopt the language and mannerisms of our parents, our siblings, and our environment. My sister, who lives in Alabama, has this crazy southern accent. And her children call me ma'am.

As a child of God, you are a citizen of the kingdom of heaven. To implement all the blessings that belong to you in the kingdom, you must learn to speak the language of God's kingdom.

In Romans 10:9, the word *confess* in Greek means "to say the same thing." Here's how you receive all God's promises in His kingdom. You read the Word of God. Believe it in your heart. Then you speak the same language, say the same thing that God says about you.

The last phrase in today's passage is *"with the mouth confession is made unto salvation."* Here's the good news: salvation includes much more than forgiveness from sin. The word *salvation* comes from the Greek word *soteria*, which means forgiveness, healing, provision, safety, restoration, rescue. For example, if you need protection, you can believe the promise in Psalm 91:9–10, and speak out this confession: "Because I have made the Lord, who is my refuge, even the Most High, my dwelling place, no evil shall befall me, nor shall any plague come near my dwelling."

God wants you to have everything you need and never lack. It is yours when you use God's formula for receiving, by faith, all He's promised you.

A Prayer for Today

Dear Father, I want my kingdom citizenship to be evident to others by how I speak and the way I act. Thank you for teaching me how to receive all You've promised so that I have all I need for an abundant life in You!

Day 4

PEACE-PROMISED CHILD OF GOD

Do not be anxious about anything, but in every situation, by prayer and petition with thanksgiving, present your requests to God. And the peace of God, which transcends all understanding, will guard your hearts and your minds in Christ Jesus.

—Philippians 4:6–7

In 2 Kings 4:8–37, there is a story about a woman who loved and worshipped God. She had blessed Elisha, the prophet, building a guest room onto her house to give him a place to stay when he came to town to preach. She was barren, so God gave her a son. But one day, the young boy died a tragic death. She had a life-and-death concern for sure! But what she did next is a powerful lesson for us. She picked up the boy and laid him on the prophet's bed and shut the door. (This is a picture of us taking our cares to Jesus.)

Then she got on her donkey and went to get the prophet. All along the way, if someone asked her how she was doing, she said, "All is well." She never spoke of death; she didn't put words to it. She would not accept it.

Instead, she spoke life, "All is well." Her faith in God gave her a different perspective on her problem. She didn't deny the facts; she just lived in the reality that God can change the facts. He brings life to dead situations.

Elisha came to the woman's home and raised her boy from the dead because this woman had shut the door on grief and death. She cast her care on the Lord. She left her son in God's hands.

Are you facing a stressful situation today that you have no idea how to fix? a worry that keeps you awake at night?

It could be a "life and death" health challenge. It could be a frightening challenge with a child, the loss of a job, or financial worries. Whatever it is, when you cast the care of it on the Lord, then you put the responsibility on Him to bring life to your dead situation.

Stress and worry never solve the problem; instead, it adds to the problem. It will make you sick. As long as you try to handle it yourself, God will let you.

Instead, shut the door on your cares and trust God. Leave your problem in your Father's skillful hands! He made the promise to you. When you give your concern to Him, you make Him responsible for solving it. Don't worry; He can handle it!

A Prayer for Today

Dear Heavenly Father, I give _____ to You today. As I lay it before You, I shut the door to this concern and leave it with You. I choose to speak "all is well" and stand on Your promises. I trust You to bring life into this dead-looking situation. I will wait on You to give me direction, and I'll obey what You show me to do through Your Word. Thank You that You provide me with peace amid this challenge.

Day 5

ALREADY-HEALED CHILD OF GOD

Let all that I am praise the Lord; may I never forget the good things he does for me. He forgives all my sins and heals all my diseases.

—Psalm 103:2–3 (NLT)

One of the most damaging religious lies to ever be perpetrated in the church is that *"God brings sickness on people to teach them a lesson."* With that kind of theology, it's no wonder people find it difficult to accept God's love for them.

So if you're wondering, *Did God bring this sickness on me to teach me a lesson?* let me help you with this one. *The answer is no!*

As a parent, would you ever devise a plan to give your child food poisoning to teach them a lesson? Or give them cancer because they are impatient and need to slow down? If you did, you would be arrested for child abuse! That would be downright evil.

Your Heavenly Father loves you much more than an earthly parent ever could. He only desires the very best for you. And He wants you well. Consistently throughout the Bible, sickness is referred to as a curse. (Read Deuteronomy 28:15–68.)

In Acts 10:38, Paul writes, *"You must have heard how God anointed him (Jesus) with the power of the Holy Spirit, of how he went about doing good and healing all who suffered from the devil's power—because God was with him."*

All sickness is from the enemy. For you to receive your healing, you need to know this truth. If you think God brought illness on you to teach you a lesson, you won't fight against it. Healing is part of your *salvation benefit package*—your inheritance as a child of God!

Note that in our scripture for today, forgiveness and healing are both in the same sentence! Just as you accept, by faith, the truth that your sins are forgiven, past, present and future, receive your healing by faith as well. It belongs to you!

A PRAYER FOR TODAY

Always loving Father, thank You that when Jesus went to the cross, He broke every curse that the enemy could ever try to throw at me. Now I only accept the blessings. I resist the enemy, and he has to flee. Holy Spirit, give me greater revelation of the truth that healing is just as much a part of my salvation as forgiveness!

Day 6

IMAGINATION-EMPOWERED CHILD OF GOD

When they knew God, they glorified him not as God,
neither were thankful; but became vain in their
imaginations, and their foolish heart was darkened.

—Romans 1:21

This may come as a surprise to you, but God gave you an imagination to help you get well!

Imagination is much more important than most people realize. The Hebrew word translated *imagination* in the Old Testament means "conception."

Napoleon Hill said this about the power of imagination: "Whatever the mind can conceive and believe, the mind can achieve."

Remember the story of Abraham? When God made a covenant with him that he would be the father of many nations, He took him outside and pointed up to the night sky and told him, "Your children will number greater than the stars in the heavens." God's illustration triggered Abraham's imagination. It helped him put God's promise into perspective and imagine what family dinners would be like at their house!

Imagination is a gift from God. Use your imagination to agree with God's Word and see yourself how God sees you: happy, healthy, and prosperous.

The Bible says in Isaiah 53:5 that *"by His stripes, you were healed."* Imagine this truth being real. (Because it is!) Most people allow their imaginations to become vain, and they agree with the image the doctors have painted rather than with the truth of the Word of God. They listen to the doctor's report, google the worst-case scenarios, and imagine themselves developing every symptom.

Instead, if you are struggling with a health issue, imagine yourself healed. When your healing manifests, what will you do first? How will you feel? Where will you go? See it in the spiritual realm, declare the promises that God has given you for your situation, and celebrate your healing. Hebrews 11:1 says, *"Now faith is the substance of things hoped for, the evidence of things not seen."* Faith is in the seeing before you see it!

Perhaps sickness is not an issue for you. Whatever concern is weighing you down today, these same principles apply.

What will your life look like when the answer manifests? Paint yourself a picture of it in your mind because God's promises never fail!

A Prayer for Today

Father, thank You for giving me an imagination. I realize I've used it negatively, seeing and expecting the worst in my situation. That is unbelief. No more! I choose to believe Your word. Holy Spirit, help me conceive in my mind and imagine all the good things my loving Father has planned for me today.

Day 7

REJECTING-UNBELIEF CHILD OF GOD

For we do not have a High Priest, who cannot sympathize with our weaknesses but was in all points tempted as we are, yet without sin.

—Hebrews 4:15

How can this verse be true? Have you ever considered the temptations of Jesus? Jesus was never married, so how could he understand the allurement of adultery? How could He have suffered the delusion of drug addiction when He never encountered cocaine? How could He have been tempted to cheat on His taxes? The IRS didn't exist back then.

But we know the whole Word of God is true, so what does the apostle Paul mean when he plainly stated, *"Jesus was tempted in all points as we are, yet without sin"*?

Hebrews 4:15 underscores the truth that our actions are not where temptation actually occurs. The root of every action starts in our thoughts, our beliefs. It is in our beliefs that we are tempted. Jesus was tempted not to believe God just as we are, but He kept believing and trusting God. He never gave in to unbelief.

All sin is rooted in unbelief. It is rejecting God's truth. Unbelief says God is not enough. Unbelief says God will not heal me. Unbelief says God will not meet my need, so I have to cheat. Unbelief says God doesn't give peace, so I need a drug fix. Unbelief says God does not love me, I have no value, so I attempt suicide. Unbelief says God didn't create me perfectly; I have female parts, but I feel like a man. I am a mistake. I need a sex change. Unbelief will take you down a road to tragedy.

In Romans 11, Paul explains to the Gentile believers how they were grafted into God's vine while the Israelites' branch had been cut off. It says in verse 23, *"God is more than ready to graft back in the natural branches when they turn from clinging to their unbelief to embracing faith."*

Are you clinging to unbelief today? Are you worried or fearful? Worry and fear are unbelief, which is sin.

Decide to believe God and His Word no matter what you see in the natural. Your faith and trust in Him will bring joy and peace regardless of the situation.

A PRAYER FOR TODAY

Heavenly Father, I refuse to cling to unbelief any longer. I choose to trust Your word that never fails. It's comforting to realize that Jesus knows just how I feel and what I am struggling with today. I will rest in You, believe You, and bask in Your peace.

Day 8

Promise-Receiving Child of God

"For I know the plans I have for you," says the Lord. "They are plans
for good and not for disaster, to give you a future and a hope."

—Jeremiah 29:11 (NLT)

Growing up, I was taught that "God will bring sickness and calamity on you to teach you a lesson." But as I've studied God's Word, I have failed to find proof of this doctrine anywhere in the Bible. It certainly wasn't Jesus' teaching method!

In Mark 4, when a great storm arose as Jesus and His disciples were in a boat on the Sea of Galilee, He did not say to His disciples, "The storm is here to teach you courage." Instead, He took authority over the storm and said, "Peace, be still!" And there was a perfect calm (Mark 4:39).

When Jesus met the widow of Nain whose only son had died, He didn't tell her that "God needed another angel in heaven." No, Jesus raised him to life and gave him back to his mother (Luke 7:14). On another occasion, Jesus' good friend Lazarus had died. He didn't tell Lazarus' sisters, "God's ways are far above our ways." No, standing outside Lazarus' tomb, He said, "Lazarus, come forth" (John 11:43)!

In every challenge, Jesus *said* something. What have you been *saying* about your situation?

When you feel pain in your body, don't blame God and say, "God allowed this pain to teach me to trust Him more." Instead, say, *"Lord Jesus, I thank You that by Your stripes I am healed"* (1 Peter 2:24). And when the checkbook balance doesn't cover the bills, don't say, "The Lord keeps me poor to keep me humble." Instead, say, *"The Lord is my shepherd; I shall not want"* (Psalm 23:1).

If you feel panic over what you hear happening in the world around you, declare God's Word. Like the psalmist, *"Thank You, Lord, that You came to deliver me from this present evil age"* (Galatians 1:4).

Don't let the devil trick you into thinking your trouble is a gift from God.

First, find out what God's Word says about your situation. *(I have included a list, "70 Promises for an Abundant Life," in the appendix of this book.)* Take the promise that fits your need. Believe it, and then open your mouth and speak it out. God's Word cannot return to Him void (Isaiah 55:11). What you believe and confess will manifest in your life!

Stand against the enemy's attack with God's promises for you, His child. You have the authority to put the devil in his place—under your feet! God loves you and wants you to live in abundance in every area of your life. Don't settle for anything less!

A PRAYER FOR TODAY

Heavenly Father, teach me to always say what You say about my life and never to accept the devil's lies. Your plan for me is always good and never evil. I hold on to Your promises for me today.

Day 9

PERFECTLY LOVED CHILD OF GOD

When you're placed into the Anointed One and joined to him, circumcision and religious obligations can benefit you nothing. All that matters now is living in the faith that is activated and brought to perfection by love.

—Galatians 5:6 (TPT)

God doesn't love you because you are good. He loves you because He is good.

The moment you received Jesus' sacrifice for your sins, you were born again and became a child of God. You were placed into the Anointed One and joined to Jesus. From the time you joined God's family, your Father's number one desire has been to lavish His love on you.

I used to think that performing religious traditions, praying long prayers, working in the church, or accomplishing a list of dos and don'ts would earn me extra credit with God so He would love and accept me and answer my prayers.

But I found out that we are loved because God is love! Matthew 10:30 says, *"So don't worry. For your Father cares deeply about even the smallest detail of your life."*

Knowing how much you are loved will produce faith in you to believe God's Word. When you know God loves you, then you will rest in His love without any fear that He won't answer your prayers. That's what it means in 1 John 4:18, *"There is no fear in love, but perfect love casts out fear."*

So how do you get a revelation of God's love for you? Ask for it. In Ephesians 3:18–19, the apostle Paul shares a prayer that he prayed, asking *for* more revelation of God's love. I challenge you to pray this prayer every day for a month and see how your understanding of God's love for you grows.

A PRAYER FOR TODAY

Heavenly Father, In Jesus' name, I ask You to give me a deeper revelation of Your love for me. I pray that I would be rooted and grounded in Your love so that I am empowered to discover what every child of God experiences—the great magnitude of the astonishing love of Christ in all its dimensions. How deeply intimate and far-reaching is Your love! How enduring and inclusive it is, endless love beyond measurement that transcends my understanding! I pray that this extravagant love pours into me until I am filled to overflowing with the fullness of God!

(Personal prayer modified from Ephesians 3:18–19 TPT)

Day 10

BLESSED-NOT-CURSED CHILD OF GOD

*The Lord will guarantee a blessing on everything you do
and will fill your storehouses with grain. The Lord, your
God, will bless you in the land he is giving you.*

—Deuteronomy 28:8

I wish you could meet my friend Dwight. Whenever he is asked "how are you?" His immediate response, accompanied by a big grin, is always "I'm too blessed to be depressed!" You'll realize how blessed you are too when you hear the good news I want to share with you today.

Deuteronomy 28 tells us of a pivotal event in the history of Moses and the Israelites. It was time for them to choose to obey or disobey God. The chapter begins with this promise: *"If you fully obey the Lord your God and carefully keep all his commands,"* then all the blessings would be theirs. But if they disobeyed, then verses 15–66 listed all the curses coming their way.

The catch was at that time, there were over six hundred laws to obey! The blessings were fantastic, but it was impossible to keep all those laws. That was God's point. He showed them that it is impossible to obey the laws and be good enough to deserve all His blessings. The law was to point them to Jesus, the Savior, who fulfilled all the law on their behalf!

In Matthew 5:17, Jesus says, *"Think not that I am come to destroy the law or the prophets: I am not come to destroy, but to fulfill."* God loves us so much that He wants us to have all His blessings and not the curses, so Jesus fulfilled the law on our behalf. Then He went one step further, and He broke all the curses too!

So now, because of Jesus, as a legitimate child of God, you can confidently receive all the blessings God promises in Deuteronomy 28, and you can legally reject every curse that the devil tries to attach to you. This makes you powerful!

Here are a few of the blessings you can expect as listed in Deuteronomy 28:3–6:

> *Blessed shall you be in the city, and blessed shall you be in the country. Blessed shall be the fruit of your body, the produce of your ground, and the increase of your herds, the increase of your cattle and the offspring of your flocks. Blessed shall be your basket and your kneading bowl. Blessed shall you be when you come in, and blessed shall you be when you go out.*
>
> *The Lord will cause your enemies who rise against you to be defeated before your face; they shall come out against you one way and flee before you seven ways.*

Read Deuteronomy 28:15–66 to see all the bad stuff you can leave behind, thanks to Jesus too! Jesus has broken every curse. Sickness, addictions, strife, and lack are all curses. Don't allow the devil to put these on you or your family—they don't belong to you.

A Prayer for Today

> *Heavenly Father, thank You that I am blessed. I am empowered to prosper every day, in every way, when I come in and when I go out—all because Jesus qualified me for blessings!*

Now stand up straight, lift your head, and say this to the devil:

I bind you, devil, and cancel all your schemes against my family and me! Get out of my house. You have no right here. In the name of Jesus!

Day 11

PLANNED-FOR-IN-ADVANCE CHILD OF GOD

You saw me before I was born. Every day of my life was recorded in your book. Every moment was laid out before a single day had passed.

—Psalm 139:16 (NLT)

Imagine this. Your Heavenly Father loves you so much that He has a journal about you! Psalm 139 says that He has written down all His dreams and plans for your life—every moment. The dictionary's definition of *moment* is "a minute portion of time." And He completed his journal about you long before your mother heard your first cry.

But here's the fascinating part: not only did He write out His dream and destiny for you, but Psalm 139 also goes on to say, *"He fashioned, or prepared, every day of my life for me ahead of time."*

This attention to detail is consistent with God's character. Isaiah 46:10 says, *"He sees the end from the beginning."*

He is Jehovah Jireh, the God Who Sees Ahead and Provides.

Here's some more good news. Because your Father already sees the destiny He has planned for you, He has also prepared the provision you will need all along the way to complete your purpose!

If you look at the world God created, it's evident that He is a God of precise order—everything in nature has an order. There is no chaos in how the earth operates. The sun rises and sets on schedule every day. The seasons change at the same time each year. Spring comes, the trees bud, new leaves soon crown the trees, then the green gives way to beautiful reds and oranges in autumn. The brilliant leaves fall to the ground signaling winter and snow, and predictably, spring blossoms again. This goes on year after year the way God planned it.

So is it any wonder that He would meticulously plan, prepare, and provide in even greater detail for His most precious and loved creation—*you*?

A Prayer for Today

Loving Father, I am overwhelmed by Your love for me. Lead me into the destiny that You have personally prepared and designed for me. I am Yours! I trust You for every step of the exciting journey we're on together.

Day 12

FAVOR-SURROUNDED CHILD OF GOD

For You, O Lord, will bless the righteous; with favor
You will surround him as with a shield.

—Psalm 5:12 (KJV)

Are you interviewing for a job today? Waiting for loan approval to start a new business? Do you desperately need your house to sell? Are you hoping to get picked for a part in the school play? Then you need favor.

Good news; as a child of God, you are promised supernatural favor!

Favor is a unique benefit promised to every child of God. Just as you favor your children over the other children in your neighborhood, your Heavenly Father favors you!

Noah believed and trusted God despite living in the midst of a very evil generation. The people on earth at that time were so wicked that God had plans to destroy them all and start over. But it says in Genesis 6:1–8 that *"Noah found favor in the sight of God."* Although God was about to pour out judgment on the whole human race, He showed favor by rescuing Noah and his family out of it all!

Joseph was a slave but found favor with Potiphar and was promoted to an executive position as overseer of his whole house. *"So Joseph found favor in his sight, and served him. Then he made him overseer of his house, and all that he had he put under his authority"* (Genesis 39:4).

Esther lived in dangerous times, similar to today, where powerful men like Haman were plotting to annihilate all the Jews. But Esther 2:15 says that *"Esther obtained favor in the sight of all who saw her."* She was favored and became queen. Then God gave her the strategy she needed to save her people.

I could go on and remind you of all the ways David experienced the favor of God. But here is the key to the favor. David boldly wrote that *"Those who seek the LORD lack no good thing"* (Psalm 34:10).

Just as Noah, Esther, Joseph, and David, discovered, when you seek the Lord, opening your heart to God's wisdom and favor, it impacts everything else in your life. Not only will He reenergize your spiritual life, but there will be a transformation of your health, finances, and relationships as well.

You receive favor the same way you received salvation; you believe in your heart that it belongs to you and speak it out of your mouth. Declare today's prayer for favor everywhere you go.

A Prayer for Today

I declare that Jesus has made me righteous, and through His covenant, I am entitled to God's favor and kindness. The favor of God surrounds me like a shield. Because of His goodness, I experience the limitless, immeasurable favor of God at all times. God's favor on me produces supernatural increase, protection, preferential treatment, provision, restoration, great victories, policies changed on my behalf, petitions granted, and conflicts won without a fight. Everywhere I go, I witness favor with both God and man!

Day 13

CHILD OF THE DOUBLE PORTION

*Instead of shame and dishonor, you will enjoy a double
share of honor. You will possess a double portion of prosperity
in your land, and everlasting joy will be yours.*

—Isaiah 61:7 (NLT)

Have you ever been misunderstood? Even worse, have you been
falsely accused? Slandered?

The enemy works overtime to try to put shame, disgrace, and
guilt on us. He often uses unsuspecting people to drive a wedge
between families and friends, husbands and wives, employers and
employees. He is all about creating division. He has undoubtedly
been working overtime in our world lately.

But as a child of God, you have special promises that you can
claim in these painful situations. Your Father gives you double for
your trouble!

Rather than get angry and vindictive, God says to forgive the
offender and leave the vengeance to Him (Romans 12:19). When
you humble yourself, seek God's help and cast your cares on Him.
You are, in essence, giving God the authority to handle the situation
for you.

"Instead of shame and dishonor, you will enjoy a double share of honor. You will possess a double portion of prosperity in your land." (Your land is your family, your job, your investments, your ministry.)

In Bible times, the double portion was the inheritance reserved for the firstborn son. But God says that as His child, because Jesus made you righteous, He commands blessings on you as if you were the firstborn son (Ezra 4:22 and Galatians 3:14)

Job is a good example. Job had become fearful and opened the door to the enemy who devastated Job's whole family. His friends falsely accused him, and his wife suggested that *"he just curse God and die."* But Job kept trusting God. He forgave his friends for their false accusations, and he honored God. Job 42:10 says, *"When Job prayed for his friends, the Lord restored his fortunes. In fact, the Lord gave him twice as much as before!"*

When you trust God to vindicate you, rectify misunderstandings and false accusations, you can expect double the blessings.

A Prayer for Today

Dear Heavenly Father, As Your "made righteous" child, I am running to you today, Lord. I am trusting You to vindicate me and restore relationships. Holy Spirit, I will listen to You as You lead me in the best way to handle what concerns me.

Day 14

CHILD OF THE WELL-PROVEN GOD

"Bring all the tithes into the storehouse, that there may be food in My house, and try Me now in this," Says the Lord of hosts, "If I will not open for you the windows of heaven and pour out for you such blessing that there will not be room enough to receive it."

—Malachi 3:10

The kingdom of God operates polar opposite to the kingdom of this world (where Satan is ruler). The world says to get rich; you need to make all the money you can and sit on the can. But in God's kingdom, wealth works on the law of sowing and reaping. Give all you can and expect a harvest!

My husband, Don, and I learned the power of tithing many years ago and have depended on it to get wealth ever since. Tithing is giving God the first 10 percent (at least) of your increase each month. Tithing declares that God is your provider, your source of everything.

Tithing is not a requirement in the new covenant, but it is a blessing we have the privilege of tapping into if we choose. God will still love you whether you tithe or not, but you limit God's ability to bless you when you hold back the tithe for yourself.

This verse in Malachi is the only place in the Bible where you'll find God daring you to test Him. We decided to take God up on His "dare" and put Him to the test.

We had a small business at the time called Midwest Shag Service. It was a specialized service we performed for a meatpacking plant in Nebraska. We had six employees who moved refrigerated trailers into the loading docks and then set them on the "ready line" for the long-haul trucking companies to hook on to the trailers and haul them to their destinations across the country so everyone could enjoy good Nebraska beef!

When we considered tithing 10 percent of our gross income, we realized that 10 percent was all we had left to live on after paying all our expenses for the company. So if we gave the tithe, we would be left with zero for a paycheck. We examined our accounts, looking for ways to increase our bottom line, but found no realistic solutions. But God said, "*Test me on this!*"

So totally as a leap of faith, we wrote the check for the tithe. As we placed it in the offering basket, we declared over it, "*This is our test, Lord. We want You to know that You are our source, our provider, and we are trusting Your word. You promise to open the windows of heaven and pour out blessings too much to contain!*"

Ten days later, Don got a call from the general manager of the meatpacking plant. He said, "I don't think you realize this, but we are doing major construction around the plant, and your drivers are doing a lot of extra work that you are not billing us for. We want to be fair with you and pay you." The increase amounted to 11 percent!

God passed the test! And He has never failed to provide for us since.

So I challenge you to trust God too. God is faithful. His kingdom works by sowing, but He even provides the seed!

2 Corinthians 9:10 reads, "*Now may He who supplies seed to the sower, and bread for food, supply and multiply the seed you have sown and increase the fruits of your righteousness.*"

The first step is, by faith, to become a sower. Start with what you have. Take the tithe out first, plant your seed, water it with the Word of God, speak 2 Corinthians 9:10 over it. You'll find out the 90 percent you have left will go farther than 100 percent when you keep it all for yourself!

A farmer doesn't plant seed and then mourn over his lost seed. No, he plants expecting a harvest!

A Prayer for Today

Father God, I never want to limit Your ability to bless me. So I'll accept Your challenge to tithe. I know you wouldn't ask me to test You if You didn't plan to prove Your faithfulness to me. I choose to trust in Your kingdom's wealth plan as you direct me to put my faith in You!

Day 15

MERCY-GRANTED CHILD OF GOD

Therefore let us [with privilege] approach the throne of grace
[that is, the throne of God's gracious favor] with confidence and
without fear, so that we may receive mercy [for our failures]
and find [His amazing] grace to help in time of need [an
appropriate blessing, coming just at the right moment].

—Hebrews 4:16 (AMP)

Sometimes we can be our own worst enemy, creating a challenging situation in our life by our own "piece of stupid" as my pastor calls it.

I used to think that if I caused the problem, I would have to deal with it on my own. How could I ask Father God to help me? After all, it was my greed, selfishness, irresponsibility, or procrastination that caused my problem.

This is where God's mercy comes into play with another benefit of the manifold grace of God. The apostle Paul tells us to come boldly to the throne of grace to find mercy even when it is our fault!

It's no wonder the Gospel is called the "almost too good to be true news!"

God's unmerited grace gives us mercy for our failures. *Unmerited* means you can't earn it. God wants to rescue you today. It's what He enjoys doing.

But He can't help you if you don't let Him.

If you are thinking, *I got myself into this mess, and I have to get myself out*, that's what God calls pride.

Mercy is part of your inheritance as a child of God.

Humbly call on your Father at the throne of grace and receive all the mercy you need today. When you do, your loving, merciful Father promises grace to provide the appropriate help at just the right time.

There's no better way to live than surrounded by your Father's mercy and grace!

A Prayer for Today

Loving Father, here's the mess I made. I don't feel like I deserve Your help, but You say You'll help me anyway! I am taking You at Your word and relying on Your grace and mercy. Father, I have to admit… Your love for me leaves me speechless!

Day 16

ANGEL-GUARDED CHILD OF GOD

What role then, do the angels have? The angels are spirit-messengers sent by God to serve those who are going to be saved.

—Hebrews 1:14 (TPT)

Are you praying for family members or friends to receive of the salvation Jesus offers to them? Are you worried something might happen to them before they accept Christ—perhaps an accident or premature death? Instead of worrying, claim God's promise to preserve and protect them.

One of my classmates at Charis Bible College told me his story of how he ended up at Bible college. He was from Hong Kong. He grew up in an impoverished Buddhist home. He relayed the amazing story of how he had come to America through a series of improbable events.

In college, some Christians gave him a Bible which he immediately threw under his bed. But finally, he heard the Gospel and got saved. Now he is in Bible School, learning the Word of God so that he can go back to Hong Kong and share the truth with others.

As I pondered God's supernatural hand on this man's life and all the obstacles he had overcome to get to America and learn about Jesus, it reminded me of this promise in Hebrews 1:14.

Because God is all-knowing, He already knows who will receive Him and become a child of God during their lifetime. How comforting to know that He assigns angels to protect those who are going to be saved. That's what happened to my friend from Hong Kong. Angels protected him until he could find the truth!

God cares about your family. Families are precious to Him. When you pray for family members and friends you love, God hears you and is at work setting up opportunities for them to turn to Him. God has also arranged for angels to guard over them until they see the truth!

A PRAYER FOR TODAY

Once again, Father, You amaze me with Your loving kindness and care over my family and me. Thank You for putting angels in charge of protecting those in my family who will be saved. I pray that You bring laborers into their path who can speak the truth in a way they will understand, accept Your gift, and be saved. In the meantime, I trust You to protect them.

Day 17

ZOE-LIFE-ENDUED CHILD OF GOD

The thief comes only in order to steal and kill and
destroy. I came that they may have and enjoy life, and
have it in abundance [to the full, till it overflows].

—John 10:10 (AMP)

Jesus could have come only to die on the cross to pay the penalty for our sins and rescue us from hell. That in itself would still have been a gift worthy of eternal praise. But God's plan was far greater than that. Jesus came that we might have and enjoy life in abundance right here on earth.

If you have one box of Cheerios that is enough, but when your whole pantry is stacked full to the top, three levels deep with Cheerios, that's abundance!

The Greek word translated life in this verse is *zoe*, and it means life in the absolute sense or *life as God has it*. Everyone who is breathing has physical life, but only those who receive Jesus as their Savior can experience life as God intended it to be. The life of God is not waiting for us when we get to heaven but is in the spirit of every born-again believer right now.

Unfortunately, most believers still live life out of their natural fleshly or soulish realm, allowing their mind, will, and emotions to dictate their life, rather than believing the Word of God and trusting God's Spirit within them.

We experience this *zoe* life by faith, trusting God's Word. Regardless of what things look like in the natural, we believe what God says about our situation. For example, God says that *by the stripes of Jesus, you were healed at the cross (Is. 53:5)*. In the physical, you may have sickness in your body, but God says you are healed. The Healer lives in you. So rather than accepting sickness and giving in to it, to live the *zoe* life, you trust God's Word and believe Him for the healing that Jesus bought for you at the cross. As you believe it in your spirit, you will see it manifest in your flesh and become a reality to you.

That's how you live in abundance!

A PRAYER FOR TODAY

Dear Heavenly Father, thank You for Your loving plan to give me abundant life—Your life here on earth. By faith, I receive everything You intend for me to have through the salvation Jesus bought for me—forgiveness, healing, prosperity, safety, restoration, and deliverance.

Day 18

Brotherly Loved Child of God

Greater love has no one than this: to lay down one's life for one's friends.

—John 15:13

For exactly eight days of my mothering career, I had a day care in my home. When a beanbag chair in the playroom got busted, and teensy, tiny, itty-bitty white balls of Styrofoam invaded every corner of my basement, I called it quits.

I asked my kids, "Who did it?" Of course, the age-old blame game ensued. Adam and Eve started it. God asked them why they were hiding after they disobeyed God and ate of the forbidden tree. Eve said the serpent made her do it. Adam pointed his finger at Eve and implied it was God's fault for making that woman in the first place!

It seems to come naturally for brothers and sisters to point the blame at each other. *But not when Jesus is your Big Brother!* He's called *"the first among many brothers and sisters"* in Romans 8:29. In Proverbs 18:24, Jesus is also called *"the Friend who sticks closer than a brother."*

We are the ones who sinned. We deserved to be blamed. But Jesus, our friend and high priest, goes to the Father and says, "I took their blame. I took their sin. They are not guilty. Here's my blood payment to prove it!"

Why would He do this? It's human nature to run and hide when you feel guilty or ashamed. You want to avoid the one you think is mad at you, just like Adam and Eve did. But God doesn't want you to hide from Him. More than anything, God's highest dream and desire is a relationship with you, and He's never mad at you!

As your faithful friend, He forgives you, He heals you, He provides for you, He protects you, He teaches you, He encourages you, and He will handle your concerns if you let Him.

Trust Him; that's what friends do!

A Prayer for Today

Lord, thank You for being my best friend. You are never too busy for me. You always have the right answers. You always keep your promises. Teach me to know You more intimately so that You are the first one I come to with my problems and concerns, not the last resort. Thank You for loving me more deeply than any earthly friend. You're my BFF (Best Friend Forever)!

Day 19

UNCONDITIONALLY LOVED
CHILD OF GOD

*But Christ proved God's passionate love for us by dying
in our place while we were still lost and ungodly!*

—Romans 5:8 (TPT)

While you were lost, mean, ugly, and ungodly, Christ died for you. That's unconditional love!

The *Webster's Dictionary* defines the word *unconditional* as "not subject to conditions or limitations."

The soldiers who mercilessly beat Jesus, mocked him, and forced him to carry His own cross were vicious and heartless, but God's love still covered them. If God loved them unconditionally, then it's safe to say there is nothing you could ever do to stop Him from loving you.

You can't earn God's love. God's unconditional love reached out to rescue you before you had done a single thing to earn it. Even before you had taken your first breath, God knew your name and loved you. Isaiah 43:1 says, *"But now, thus says the Lord, who created you, O Jacob, and He who formed you, O Israel: 'Fear not, for I have redeemed you; I have called you by your name; You are Mine.'"*

Think of this: before you had accomplished anything for God—actually, before you were even born—God had you on His mind. He saw you and loved you so much that He wrote down His dream for your life. Psalm 139:16 says, *"Your eyes saw my substance, being yet unformed. And in Your book they all were written, the days fashioned for me, when as yet there were none of them. How precious also are Your thoughts to me, O God! How great is the sum of them!"*

God doesn't love you because you are good. God loves you because He is good—and He is Love.

You are loved unconditionally by God Almighty. This simple but profound truth is the foundational key to understanding your identity as a child of God. Knowing God's unconditional love for you will change your attitude, give you confidence, give you boldness, and strengthen your faith to believe God's promises to you.

God said it—so believe it. You are *loved!*

A Prayer for Today

Dear loving Father, although I cannot fully grasp how You can love me as You do, You've proven it time and time again. So I choose to accept Your unconditional love the only way I possibly can—by faith. Thank you for loving me.

Day 20

CHILD OF THE PROMISE-KEEPING GOD

For all of God's promises find their "yes" of fulfillment in him. And as his "yes" and our "amen" ascend to God, we bring him glory!

—2 Corinthians 1:20 (TPT)

What do you need today? Healing? Provision? Wisdom? Favor on your job? A debt paid off? Protection? In both the Old and New Testaments, hundreds of promises cover every single need you could possibly have.

When God sent Jesus to earth, He said yes to all the promises for you. And here's the excellent news: Jesus qualified you to receive them all!

Jesus is the fulfillment of the law (Matthew 5:17). Jesus kept the law on your behalf. Your Heavenly Father is not answering yes based on your goodness but based on Jesus' goodness. That's grace!

So since God has already answered yes to your request, you can stop begging Him!

The apostle Paul emphasizes this in Romans 8:31, "*What then shall we say to these things? If God is for us, who can be against us?*" Your Father God is on your side. You plus God make a majority. God has already said yes, now it's your turn to agree with the promise.

Your response according to 2 Corinthians 1:20 must be "amen!" which means "so be it." In other words, you agree with God. You believe that what God says is yours—really is yours! That's called faith.

God gives us even more assurance of His deep desire in Romans 8:32 (TPT), *"For God has proved his love by giving us his greatest treasure, the gift of his Son. And since God freely offered him up as the sacrifice for us all, he certainly won't withhold from us anything else he has to give."*

When you believe God is your Promise-Keeping God, and you declare "amen—so be it," it brings God glory. Why? Because He loves to lavish His love on you and give you what you are believing for—it makes Him look good!

He wants to meet your needs today. I hope you'll say, "Amen to that!"

A Prayer for Today

Heavenly Father, Your love for me is beyond my comprehension. I believe Your promises are for me right now. Thank You that Jesus qualified me to receive every promise guaranteed. You've already said yes, so I say, "Amen."

See the appendix to this book for my list of "70 Promises for an Abundant Life." *You can say "amen" to these!*

Day 21

PEACE-RULED CHILD OF GOD

And let the peace (soul harmony which comes) from Christ rule (act as umpire continually) in your hearts [deciding and settling with finality all questions that arise in your minds, in that peaceful state] to which as [members of Christ's] one body you were also called [to live].

—Colossians 3:15 (AMP)

Have you ever had a big decision to make and felt unsure what to do?

While I was attending Charis Bible College, I was diagnosed with macular degeneration. With this eye disease, straight lines look crooked. After hearing the diagnosis, I began claiming the promise that *"God goes before me and makes the crooked places straight"* (Isaiah 45:2).

The medical treatment for this disease is a monthly injection in my eyeball to help stop the disease from progressing. However, since claiming God's healing promises, my eyesight was improving, and the lines were straightening out!

So my big decision was whether to keep my next appointment with the retina specialist for another injection in my eye. Do I obey the doctor? Or trust the word of the Healer who lives inside me?

As I debated this decision on my way to school this particular morning, I prayed that the Holy Spirit would make it clear to me what I should do. Immediately I thought, *I wish I could talk to Melva.* Melva was the lady at our church who had initially agreed with me for the healing in my eyes. She is also a graduate of Charis Bible College.

It was my usual routine to get to school at about 6:30 a.m. to get a good parking spot and have time to study and pray before classes begin. I had a quiet place that I liked to sit upstairs and far down at the end of the hall where I could be alone. I was sitting there that morning when all of a sudden, I noticed someone sitting nearby—it was Melva! She didn't attend classes anymore, so it was unusual for her to be there. I believe the Holy Spirit brought her there for me.

After I recovered from the shock of seeing her, I told her about the decision I had to make about keeping my eye appointment. She asked me just one question, "Where do you have peace, in going to the doctor or not?"

God used her to remind me always to be led by peace. *"Let peace be the umpire,"* it says in Colossians 3:15.

Immediately, I realized that I had peace in *not* keeping the appointment. My only fear was in what the doctor would say. We must always be led by peace and not by fear. Everyone's situation is different. I am not saying that you shouldn't see a doctor. Follow what gives you peace.

When you let peace rule in your heart, it will move you to the right decision every time.

A PRAYER FOR TODAY

Dear Father, thank You for giving me Your Holy Spirit who will always lead me with peace. You are not hiding Your plans from me. As I ask You for direction, You are faithful to guide me. I trust You because You love me and are always on my side.

Day 22

PRIVILEGED CHILD OF GOD

*Behold what manner of love the Father has bestowed
on us, that we should be called children of God!*

—1 John 3:1a

Once you've accepted Jesus as your Savior and the Lord of your
life, then you are officially a child of God. I hope by now you
realize what a privilege it is to be included in the family of God.

God Almighty, Jehovah Jireh, the Great I Am, the One Who
Spoke the Universe into Existence, the God of All Peace, the Good
Shepherd claims *you* as His very own child! You are part of His
Family. He is the perfect Father and takes supernaturally good care
of His children.

However, the devil is always trying his best to get you to forget
your identity. He wants you to settle for a life in the pits, far below
what your Father has made available and desires for you. So it is
important to keep reminding yourself who your Father is, who He
says you are, and what He says belongs to you as His child.

So today, I want to remind you how awesome your Father says
you are. Here are just a few truths about you:

- Even before the world was created, you were planned. *"Just
  as He chose us in Him before the foundation of the world, that*

we should be holy and without blame before Him in love"
(Ephesians 1:4).

- You have been made acceptable to God. *"Therefore, since we have been made righteous through His faithfulness combined with our faith, we have peace with God through our Lord Jesus Christ" (Romans 5:1).*

- You are an heir in Christ. *"And if children then heirs, heirs of God and joint heirs with Christ, if indeed we suffer with Him, that we may also be glorified together with Him" (Romans 8:17).*

- You lack no good thing. *"The young lions do lack and suffer hunger, but those who seek the Lord shall not lack any good thing" (Psalm 34:10).*

- You have an abundance for every good work. *"And God is able to make all grace abound toward you that you always having all sufficiency in all things, may have an abundance for every good work" (2 Corinthians 9:8).*

- You were predestined by God for success. *"And we know that all things work together for good to those who love God, to those who are the called according to His purpose. For whom He foreknew, He also predestined to be conformed to the image of His Son, that He might be the first born among many brethren" (Romans 8:28–30).*

The creator of the universe, your Father, loves you with an everlasting love!

A PRAYER FOR TODAY

Loving Father, thank You for giving me more and more revelation of Your love for me. I receive it! What a privilege to have you as my Father. It's not every kid that can say their Dad created the universe!

Day 23

COMPLETELY WHOLE CHILD OF GOD

But He was wounded for our transgressions, He was bruised for our iniquities; the chastisement for our peace was upon Him, and by His stripes, we are healed.

—Isaiah 53:5

Have you ever opened a gift with lots of tissue paper and assumed there was just one gift, but the giver said, "Wait, there's more! Dig deeper in the tissue, and you'll find some more gifts."

Many people stop opening the gift from Jesus too soon. They believe that Jesus' gift was only to pay the penalty for their sins so they can be forgiven and get into heaven in "the sweet bye and bye."

But God's gift for you goes way beyond that! He desires abundant life for you right now. Because He loves you with unconditional, endless love, His gift of salvation includes everything you need for your life today—not just a ticket to heaven.

The Hebrew word for *peace* in our verse for today is *shalom* which means *"to make complete or whole, nothing missing, nothing broken; complete welfare, health, prosperity and peace."*

So at the same time that Jesus paid the penalty for your sins, He also gave you healing, provision, and peace. It's all part of Jesus' gift!

Instead of sickness, Jesus' gift includes healing. Psalm 103:3 says, *"He forgives all my sins and heals all my diseases."*

Instead of lack, His gift includes provisions and the power to get wealth. In 2 Corinthians 9:10, it says, *"Now may He who supplies seed to the sower, and bread for food, supply and multiply the seed you have sown and increase the fruits of your righteousness."*

Instead of anxiety, His gift includes peace. You can believe God's Word and rest in Him to bring you out of worry and discouragement. In Psalm 40:1–2 David writes this about a time of discouragement in his life: *"I waited patiently for the Lord; and He inclined to me, and heard my cry. He also brought me up out of a horrible pit, out of the miry clay, and set my feet upon a rock, and established my steps."*

Don't permit the enemy to steal the gifts Jesus offers you. Jesus paid dearly for every one of them. Unwrap and enjoy every gift!

A PRAYER FOR TODAY

Heavenly Father, I keep pulling out the tissue and finding more and more special gifts! Thank You for Your all-encompassing salvation. You forgave all my sin—past, present and future—plus You've broken the curses of sickness, poverty, and anxiety from off of me too. You made me whole! Jesus, You are my Savior and Lord. I choose to believe Your Word and trust You today.

Day 24

WELL-SHEPHERDED CHILD OF GOD

The Lord is my Shepherd, I shall not want.

—Psalm 23:1

David, the shepherd boy who became king, was referred to by God as *"a man after God's own heart."* There's so much we can learn from David's life and the psalms that he penned as he watched over his flock of sheep.

Did you know that David prophesied about Jesus, the Messiah, in Psalm 22, 23, and 24? These psalms were written one thousand years before Jesus' birth!

In Psalm 22, David prophesies about Jesus our Redeemer-Savior. Psalm 24 looks ahead to Jesus, our Coming King. For the next several days, I want to focus on the well-known Psalm 23. It is a prophecy about Jesus as our Lord—right now as a present-day reality. Psalm 23 is written from the sheep's perspective and is packed full of promises that you can claim 24/7.

Psalm 23:1 begins with the declaration: *"The Lord is my Shepherd, I shall not want."*

David could speak from experience about shepherding. He spent many cold, lonely nights caring for sheep. He knew it was his responsibility as a shepherd to meet every possible need of the sheep, for they were helpless on their own.

Do you realize that when you make Jesus your Lord, He takes over the responsibility of being your Shepherd? However, His promise goes beyond your need. He promises that when you trust Him as your Lord, *"you will not lack for any good thing."*

Psalm 34:10 says it this way, *"Even strong, young lions sometimes go hungry, but those who trust in the Lord will lack no good thing."*

God even told Job, in the oldest book in the Bible, to *"get to know God and you will have plenty of silver"* (Job 22:21–25)!

So the first step in living the blessed and prosperous life that your Father dreams for you is to declare that Jesus is your Savior and Lord.

If you have not accepted the gift of salvation, I encourage you to do it today. (There is a sample prayer for salvation in the front of this book.)

Believe God to not only save you from sin but to be your Good Shepherd too. Expect to see His provision in your life every day.

A PRAYER FOR TODAY

Thank You, Lord, for being my Good Shepherd!
With You as my Shepherd, I will not lack any good thing.
Lead me in the way I should go to find the provision You
have prepared for me. I am trusting in You.

Day 25

GPS-Led Child of God

*He makes me to lie down in green pastures; He leads me
beside the still waters. He restores my soul; He leads me
in the paths of righteousness for His name's sake.*

—Psalm 23:2–3

I don't know how we ever lived without GPS. The last time I remember using a paper map, I flew into Pennsylvania with my mother for a family wedding. We rented a car, then tried to find our way to the rehearsal dinner. In downtown Philadelphia, I stopped at a gas station, unfolded the four-foot-wide map on the hood of the car and tried to pinpoint where we were at and where we needed to go. We were totally lost and arrived an hour late to our destination.

But what I appreciate even more than the GPS on our phones today is being "Guided Personally by the Spirit" kind of GPS!

In Psalm 23:2–3, David continues describing the life of a child of God (the sheep) with our Lord as our Shepherd—our Guide.

I heard a tour guide from Israel explain that "the paths of righteousness" are actually the well-worn dirt paths that wind in a spiral up the hills in the sheep's pasture. The paths go to the peak of the hill so the sheep can stand on the top and see for miles. So I like to pray, *"Thank You, Lord, that You lead me in paths of righteousness all the way to the top!"*

If you have made Jesus your Lord, then He is your Shepherd who wants to be your tour guide in life. He'll guide you around danger, to the best pastures (places of provision), and to the still water (peaceful places).

It is dangerous for sheep to drink from a rushing river. If their wool gets soaked, they can fall in the water and drown. They need calm water. Following the Shepherd will keep you safe.

Learn to listen to your Shepherd. He will guide you to fulfill your destiny. Psalm 37:23 says, *"The steps of a good man are ordered by the Lord, and He delights in his way."*

A Prayer for Today

Lord, I am so glad that You are my Shepherd and that I have GPS! I am Guided Personally by Your Spirit. Knowing that You are leading me in the way I should go, I rest in You today. Thank You that You lead me to the top! Teach me to listen carefully to You and follow Your directions. I know Your plan is better than anything I could dream of on my own.

Day 26

PEACE-PROMISED CHILD OF GOD

He leads me beside still waters; He restores my soul.

Psalm 23:2–3

David continues in Psalm 23, describing with great passion how the Lord, our Shepherd, watches over and cares for us, His children—His sheep.

When my grandson, Jackson, was five years old, he was memorizing Psalm 23 for school. As he was quoting the psalm, he stopped and asked me, "Grammie, what does it mean that 'He restores my soul'?"

I explained to him that sheep wool attracts a lot of dirt, mud, sticks, briars, and manure as they graze in the pasture. Sheep can get so loaded down with gunk that they become top-heavy. Then they fall over, legs in the air, and can't get up! (The term is becoming *cast*.) If the shepherd doesn't come quickly, clean their wool, and set them back on their feet, they will die.

Drawing on my creative resources, I made up a little game to explain it to him.

I pretended to be the shepherd, and he was the sheep. He crawled around on the floor like a little lamb. Then he would fall over on his back, put his feet in the air and cry, "Bah-bah, help me, help me! I've fallen, and I can't get up!" As the shepherd, I would hurry to the lamb, pretend to clean him up, set him back on his feet, and hold him between my legs until he was stable and could walk again. Over and over and over again, we played our little game.

Pondering our humorous little parody, I realized it taught a profound spiritual principle.

We can get so burdened down with cares of this world (worry), mud (sin), manure and briars (offenses and hurts) that we fall and can't get up. The best thing to do is call out to Jesus, our Shepherd, who restores our soul and gives us His peace. And just like in the game with Jackson, no matter how many times we fall over, our Shepherd is always merciful and willing to clean us up and set us back on our feet again!

A PRAYER FOR TODAY

Dear Father, thank You for being my Good Shepherd. I refuse to allow cares, worry, hurts, and offenses to knock me off my feet. I give those all to You. Thank You for cleaning me up, setting me free, and for giving me Your peace as I trust in You.

Day 27

FULLY PROTECTED CHILD OF GOD

Yea, though I walk through the valley of the shadow of death, I will fear
no evil; for You are with me; Your rod and Your staff, they comfort me.

—Psalm 23:4

As a prize for memorizing the Twenty-Third Psalm in Sunday
school, I received a charm bracelet engraved with the psalm. But
it wasn't until I was an adult that I realized that this psalm of David
was describing the reality that we, as children of God, are meant to
live every single day of our life.

We've already looked at the truths in Psalm 23:1–3 that the
Lord is our Shepherd who is our Provider, Guide, and Peace. In verse
4, our Shepherd is our Protector.

When Jesus told the parable of the Good Samaritan, He said,
*"a man was going down from Jerusalem to Jericho and was attacked by
thieves"* (Luke 10:30). This stretch of road was known as the valley of
the shadow of death—a dangerous place to travel.

David was essentially saying, even in the most dangerous situation you can think of, there is no reason to fear because your Shepherd
is with you to protect you. He is with you because He loves you!

So how can you be assured of safety and victory every time? It
says in verse 4, *"Your rod and Your staff, they comfort me."* The rod
and staff represent the Word of God and the Holy Spirit. When you

stay close to your Shepherd, following His Word and listening to the Holy Spirit instruct you in the way you should go, you will not need to fear.

You can rest in the comfort of knowing you have the full force of heaven as your inheritance—at your beck and call! Psalm 91:15 promises, *"When he calls out to me, I will answer him. I will be with him when he is in trouble; I will rescue him and bring him honor."*

On your own, this world can be a scary place to live these days, but don't allow fear to take over. Fear will keep you from receiving the promises. Stay in faith, believing and accepting God's promises for you.

A PRAYER FOR TODAY

Thank You, Father, for Your promise of protection. I will not fear. I choose to trust in You. You will bring me through in victory!

Day 28

FEASTING-IN-VICTORY CHILD OF GOD

You prepare a feast before me in plain sight of my enemies.

—Psalm 23:5a (NET)

I am a huge football fan. My family loves cheering for the Nebraska Cornhuskers. We had high hopes for a championship season this year, but we're starting to have our doubts. However, here's a victory you can count on: as a child of God, you are already declared the winner before the game is even played! Jesus won the victory for you!

When the children of Israel, led by Joshua, finally arrived in the promised land, God assured them that there would be battles to fight. He also told them that as long as they trusted Him and didn't try to fight on their own, that they would be the winners every time.

Joshua 1:6 says, *"Be strong, and of good courage, for to this people you shall divide as an inheritance the land which I swore to their fathers to give them."* God had already declared to the Israelites that this land belonged to them; it was their inheritance.

It's the same way for you today too as a child of God. You've already been declared the winner!

. As we've been reading in Psalm 23, when you trust the Lord, your Shepherd, you shall not lack, *and* He will prepare a feast for you in the presence of your enemies.

Yes, we have enemies in this world. But your Shepherd will see to it that you come out a winner when you put your faith in Him!

God loves to lavish his favor on His kids and make the world envious. Not only will you come out on top, but the Shepherd will prepare a feast for you to celebrate, causing your enemies to be green with envy when they see just how well God provides for and defends His children.

Are you facing a battle today? Don't fight it on your own. Look to Jesus and believe what He promises you. Victory is part of your inheritance!

Rest in Jesus. Then get out your fork to dig into the feast prepared for you.

A Prayer for Today

Father God, thank You for giving me Your Word so that I can have perfect peace and confidence in You. I know that in the world, I will encounter tribulation and trials and distress and frustration; but I choose to take courage, I have confidence that you have already overcome the world, and deprived it of power to harm me. So I will not be afraid but will trust in You. (Based on John 16:33)

Day 29

ANOINTED CHILD OF GOD

You anoint my head with oil; my cup runs over.

—Psalm 23:5b

When David was a shepherd, it was the common practice in those days to anoint the sheep by pouring oil on their heads. This created a protective covering over the sheep from lice and other insects that would try to burrow into the ears and wool of the sheep. Anointing the sheep would make the wool slippery so the insects would slide off. This practice was critical in keeping the sheep healthy.

Biblically, anointing the head with oil symbolizes protection, promotion, blessing, and empowerment. The *head* is symbolic of leadership or authority. Just like how the sheep's head needed protection from bugs and insects, our head needs protection from the lies of the enemy and the temptations all around us.

As a child of God, you are anointed with the oil of the Holy Spirit. The Holy Spirit empowers you with godly wisdom to make good decisions which result in protection, blessings, promotions, and power in your life.

Then David goes on to say, *"My cup runs over,"* a picture of abundance, more than enough provision. Just like Jesus said, He came to give us life abundantly (John 10:10)!

The Lord, your Shepherd, desires for you to experience all His goodness, an overabundant, more-than-enough supply of provision, plus protection, promotions, and power. Don't live in lack today when you are destined to a life overflowing with abundance!

Believe His Word, apply it in your life, and receive all He has for you today.

A Prayer for Today

Father, life is good with You as my Shepherd! Thank You for anointing my head with the oil of the Holy Spirit. You give me wisdom, guide me, protect me, bless me, and promote me. I accept Your overflowing provision. You are right. I will never lack with You as my Shepherd!

Day 30

GOODNESS-AND-MERCY-ENGULFED CHILD OF GOD

*Surely, only goodness, mercy, and unfailing love
shall follow me all the days of my life,*

—Psalm 23:6a (AMP)

David brings Psalm 23 to a close with a dynamic crescendo expressing your Heavenly Father's love for you, dear child of God. God loves you so intensely that He follows you around with goodness, mercy, and unfailing love everywhere you go. This is the reality that every child of God is ordained to live in every single day.

Expect good! Expect favor! Expect mercy! Expect special treatment!

But beware of the enemy's schemes against you. The devil will try to get under your skin and throw bad stuff at you. It's critical that you recognize where the bad things come from so you can refuse them in your life.

In John 10:10, Jesus tells us who is behind everything bad. I like how the Passion Translation says this:

A thief has only one thing in mind—he wants to steal, slaughter, and destroy. But I have come to give you everything in abundance, more than you expect—life in its fullness until you overflow! (TPT)

Here's the bottom line: God is good. The devil is bad.

James 4:7 (TPT) tells us what to do when the enemy tries to steal from us with sickness, lack, financial problems, relational problems, accidents, etc. It says, *"So then, surrender to God. Stand up to the devil and resist him and he will turn and run away from you."*

How do you stand up to the devil? Enforce the promises. It's not enough to know the truth; you must speak the Word of God out loud.

Your Father promises that goodness, mercy, and unfailing love belong to you. It's part of your inheritance. It follows you around everywhere you go.

So be on your guard and enforce your inheritance today!

A Prayer for Today

Heavenly Father, thank You that Your goodness and mercy follow me all day long today. I expect to see it everywhere I go and in everything I do. I put the devil on notice: I will not tolerate your schemes against me or my family. Take your hands off. I am a child of God!

Day 31

CHILD OF GOD, FOREVER RESIDING IN FATHER'S HOUSE

And I will dwell in the house of the Lord forever.

—Psalm 23:6b

David's description in Psalm 23 of the present-day realities of the blessed and favored life of the child of God comes to this conclusion: life is so good as God's child you'll want to move right in to Father's house and stay forever!

So far, in Psalm 23, we've learned that Jesus is your Shepherd, your Provider, your Guide, your Peace, your Protector. And now we see that He is our Inheritance.

As a child of God your destiny is to dwell in Father's house forever—for all eternity, never to be separated from Him again.

But here's the exciting part—eternity starts now, here on earth.

In Bible times, as the homeowner, you were responsible for the guests in your home. Your responsibility was to meet *all* the needs of your guest as long as they were under your roof.

Well, guess what? In God's house, there is wealth and great abundance. He makes his driveway out of gold! So there is no lack at the Lord's table. He cares for you continually as your Good Shepherd.

First Peter 5:7 says, *"Casting the whole of your care [all your anxieties, all your worries, all your concerns once and for all] on Him, for He cares for you affectionately and cares about you watchfully."*

The glorious life of the child of God described in Psalm 23 is the result of your decision to do only two things—believe and declare, "The Lord is my Shepherd."

The life promised in Psalm 23 is not a reward for good behavior and keeping a list of dos and don'ts. Instead, it is a gift of God's grace through Jesus' blood. It is the result of having a relationship with God—trusting Him to be your Shepherd.

A Prayer for Today

Dear Father, thank You for loving me so much that You've invited me to live in Your house forever. I accept! I declare that You are my Shepherd. I will follow You, trust You, and believe Your Word. When I trust You and receive all Your goodness, it shows the world how much my Shepherd loves me and how well You care for me. I love You too.

Day 32

CHILD OF THE ALWAYS FAITHFUL GOD

*Do not be anxious about anything, but in every situation, by prayer
and petition, with thanksgiving, present your requests to God.*

—Philippians 4:6

Growing up in Nebraska, I loved autumn. It's the time of year
when God shows off His creativity of colors, turning the leaves
to bright oranges and red, just because He can. It's the time when
the cornfields are bursting with full heads of corn and waiting for
the reapers. It's harvest time, the traditional time we think of giving
thanks for God's abundance.

But the apostle Paul taught we should be thankful all year long.
As we see in Philippians 4:6, "thanksgiving" is the catalyst to keep
us from being anxious or worried. Thanksgiving causes us to focus
on all the ways the Lord has blessed us and been faithful to us in the
past, assuring us of His faithfulness this time too.

When Moses was leading the children of Israel on their journey
across the desert to the promised land, there were several times that
God instructed Moses to pile up rocks where they had witnessed
God's faithfulness (Joshua 4). In the future, when they saw that pile
of stones, it would remind them to tell their children the story of
what happened there.

Can you imagine Moses talking to his great-grandchildren? "Hey kids, do you see this huge pile of rocks? We're standing right on the very spot where Jehovah God parted the Red Sea, and we all walked through on dry ground. It was a miracle! The good news is that God never changes. He is always faithful and good!"

Psalm 9:1 says, *"I will praise you, Lord, with all my heart; I will tell of all the marvelous things you have done."*

Life gets busy. Over time, it's easy to forget those miraculous answers to prayers we witnessed in our past. How faithful He has been to keep His promises to us!

I challenge you today to make a list of answered prayers. Remember the victories, provisions, and miracles that God has lavished upon you, His child.

Remembering His faithfulness helps to reinforce your confidence that your Father will come through for you this time too. It soothes your worries and calms your fears.

He is a faithful God. He's not about to fail you now!

A PRAYER FOR TODAY

Heavenly Father, I call on You, and You answer me. Thank You for Your faithfulness every single time. You never change, so You will continue to be faithful to me now. I will praise You with my whole heart and refuse to worry for You are my God.

Day 33

CHILD OF GOD WHO'S ALREADY GOT IT

According as his divine power hath given unto us all things
that pertain unto life and godliness, through the knowledge
of him that hath called us to glory and virtue.

—2 Peter 1:3

What are you trying to get God to do for you today? Do you need healing? Could you use some favor on your job? Do you need extra money to pay an unexpected bill?

The truth is, you don't need to get God to do anything for you. He has already done it. You've already got it!

The only thing you are lacking is knowledge on how to receive what's already been provided.

Think back to your sixteenth birthday. Let's imagine that during your party, your father walks up to you, gives you a big hug, and drops in your hand the keys to a brand-new sports car. He says, "Your new car is parked in the garage!"

While holding this shiny key in your hand, would you respond to your Dad by saying "Oh, Dad, please give me a new car. I'm sixteen now, just got my driver's license, and I really need a car. This isn't a selfish request. I'll tell everyone this car came from you. Please, Dad, please give me a car"?

Of course not! You'd say "Thanks, Dad!" then take off running to the garage and hop in your new car. You would have the faith in your dad that the car was really in the garage, simply because he said so.

But most churchgoing people, even though the Word plainly tells them what Jesus has already done for them, keep begging God to give them what He's already told them they have.

The Bible says in Ephesians 1:3, *"Blessed be the God and Father of our Lord Jesus Christ, who hath blessed us with all spiritual blessings in heavenly places in Christ."*

Paul says, *He "hath blessed us with all spiritual blessings."* That's past tense. It's already done. You already have all spiritual blessings.

God is a spirit. God has already provided everything you need in the spiritual realm; using your faith and believing what God said, you bring it into the physical realm.

It is not a matter of trying to get God to move in your life; it's a matter of you moving into agreement with Him and receiving what He has already provided.

A Prayer for Today

Dear Father, You are a good, good Father to see ahead and prepare for me everything I will ever need. By faith, I take You at Your word and receive all the blessings you have planned for me.

Day 34

NEVER-ALONE CHILD OF GOD

Be strong and of good courage, do not fear nor be afraid
of them; for the Lord your God, He is the One who goes
with you. He will not leave you nor forsake you.

—Deuteronomy 31:6

My husband and I had the pleasure of experiencing the world premiere performance of *David, the King of Jerusalem*, at Charis Bible College.

The life of David was beautifully reenacted from his early childhood, his anointing as king, through his years as a shepherd, killing Goliath, finally occupying the throne in Israel, through victories and defeats, his sin with Bathsheba and, finally, at the end of his life, passing on the crown to his son Solomon.

What impacted me most from the performance—David was never alone. God, in the form of the Holy Spirit, was with him in every scene. He stayed right beside him everywhere he went.

The Holy Spirit (portrayed as the man in white who always looked at David with sincere love in his eyes) would whisper the Word of God to David for guidance, encouragement, and warnings. He showed love, care, and acceptance for David regardless of the direction he chose.

What a profound demonstration of the promise of God to His beloved children, for He Himself has said, "I will never leave you nor forsake you."

Picture this: as a child of God, you have God with you always, holding your hand. *"I will strengthen you and help you. I will hold you up with my victorious right hand,"* it says in Isaiah 41:10.

But since Jesus died and rose again, you have an even closer connection than David had. The Holy Spirit is not just right beside you but *in you*, guiding you, comforting you, encouraging you, opening doors of opportunity to you.

I encourage you to meditate on this today: having received Jesus Christ as your Savior, God is in you!

God is with you on your job, in that sales presentation, raising your children, driving your car, cooking dinner, always everywhere you go today and every day.

Expect to hear His voice. Listen and follow Him.

A Prayer for Today

Heavenly Father, thank You for Your promise to be with me always. How wonderful to have the assurance that You will never, ever leave me. Teach me to hear Your voice and follow You.

Day 35

Employing-the-But Child of God

*I have told you these things, so that in Me you may have [perfect]
peace and confidence. In the world, you have tribulation and trials
and distress and frustration, but be of good cheer [take courage, be
confident, certain, undaunted]! For I have overcome the world. [I have
deprived it of power to harm you and have conquered it for you.]*

—John 16:33 AMP

In my Bible, this scripture is in red letters. Jesus said it. And it's a
promise.

I'm sure you'll agree with me; we are living in tribulations and
trials that Ward and June Cleaver would never have imagined back
in the days of "Leave It to Beaver." A pandemic, mask mandates,
shutdowns, election fraud, devastating storms, a border crisis, and
more. It is like nothing we've ever endured before in our lifetime.
However, there is a small three-letter word in this scripture that
changes everything—*but.*

When the word *but* is inserted in a sentence, it nullifies the pre-
vious statement. And in John 16:33, this is a big *but!*

On Jesus' side, you can take courage, be confident, certain, and
undaunted. That's a good word for today. God's overcoming victory
is greater than the trials in this world. *God has deprived it of the power*

to harm you. That means you can live above it all, be on top and not the bottom when you believe and trust in God's Word and promises.

My husband and I decided not to participate in the pandemic scare. We are citizens in the Kingdom of God, so we chose to live in peace and not fill our minds with constant bad news and propaganda, which promotes fear. We turned off the news. Philippians 4:8 says to *"think on things that are of good report."* So, we get our news from truthful news sources like Victory News, which is found at govictory.com.

We go to a church where we have the freedom to shake hands, hug our brothers and sisters in Christ, sing and worship mask-free (thanks to the Supreme Court's recent decision upholding the First Amendment.) It's interesting to note that several people had the coronavirus in our church, but it was only serious in a couple of cases. Everyone recovered, and we declared as a church family that the *"curse could not come again"* (Nahum 1:9). We keep our focus on the Word of God and His truth. Our whole congregation declares in church every Sunday that "this is a perfect health zone!" We claim God's promises as our own and stand in faith to receive them, and we enjoy His peace and perfect health. Like it says in John 16:33, *"He conquered the world for us!"*

Which side of the *but* are you living on today? It's the choice of two kingdoms.

Choose to live in the Kingdom of God by believing and trusting Him to take care of you. Jesus says in John 17:16, *"We are in the world, but we are not of the world."* There's another *but!*

A Prayer for Today

Heavenly Father, I choose to live in your Kingdom. Your promises keep me in joy and peace even amid tribulation all around me. I embrace living life with Jesus by my side!

Day 36

VIP Child of God

*See what [an incredible] quality of love the Father has given
(shown, bestowed on) us, that we should [be permitted to] be named
and called and counted the children of God! And so we are!*

—1 John 3:1 AMP

God has only one requirement for adoption into His family: accepting Jesus Christ as your Savior and Lord. As a child of God, a member of God's own family, you have exclusive privileges and 24/7 access to your Father. Are you taking advantage of your family member status?

Religion teaches such a holy reverence for God that in many churches, their ritualistic treatment of God makes Him seem unapproachable, uncaring, and distant. Yes, He is Holy, Almighty, Creator, Supreme overall, and should be revered, of course. But first of all, He is Father to His children.

As much as President Trump loves Americans and is personable and friendly on stage, you would still have to go through specific protocol to have a chance at a private meeting with him. But his family has immediate access to him anytime they want. When his children call, he will interrupt his meetings to speak with them. Although, as leader of the free world, his job was protecting the security and prosperity of the United States, he is keenly aware that his first responsibility is to his family. Ivanka, Don Jr, and Barron don't have to observe certain forms of etiquette or approach him timidly. He's their dad, they respect him, but they come to him with confidence knowing they are welcome anytime.

Are you genuinely viewing God as your Father today—as your perfect Father who loves you with all-encompassing, unconditional love? Or do you see Him foremost as Holy, Almighty God, El Elyon, Creator God? While He is all that and more, His first responsibility is to you—His child!

The next time you pray and talk to God, check your attitude. Ask yourself—how do I feel about my conversation with God? Does He seem distant? Too holy to approach? Do I feel like I have to beg? Do I feel timid in approaching Him? Am I fearful He won't come through for me? If so, you need a more profound revelation of your Father's love. Understanding His perfect love for you casts out fear (1 Jn 4:18), so you can come boldly to Daddy for anything you need.

A Prayer for Today

Dear Father, Your Son, Jesus, is the One and only One, who has qualified me to be your child. So I'm asking you to give me more revelation of the height and depth and width and breadth of your love for me. Help me to view you as my loving Father first and Almighty God second.

Day 37

Designed-to-Live-Carefree Child of God

Casting all your care upon Him, for He cares for you.

—1 Peter 5:7

God boldly declared that the creation of man and woman was God's most exceptional work of all time. When God spoke into existence the sun and moon, day and night, seas and dry land, vegetation, fish, and animals, after each creation, He said, "It was good."

But when He looked at the man and woman He created, He boasted, "It was very good!" The human body is spectacular. God equipped us with everything we need to sustain our life—a blood-filtering system, oxygen system, ventilation, built-in GPS, digestive system, eyes and ears, and a broadcasting system to declare the Word of God and to create with our words. But one glaring omission to His creation was a mechanism to handle stress. Was this a blatant oversight in His meticulously detailed creation plan?

According to the American Psychological Association, reoccurring stress is linked to the six leading causes of death: heart disease, cancer, lung ailments, accidents, and cirrhosis of the liver. More than 75 percent of all doctor visits are for stress-related ailments and complaints.

God did not create your body to handle stress for one reason: *He planned to take care of the stress for you!*

But He does give you a choice:

- *Choice number 1*—you can go it alone and try to handle things on your own. (Hint: when you choose this option, He calls this pride.)
- *Choice number 2*—you can humble yourself and trust God. Give Him your worries and problems because He cares for you.

Rather than a stress-handling mechanism, He created you with a "casting mechanism."

First Peter 5:7, in the Amplified translation, says, *"Casting the whole of your care [all your anxieties, all your worries, all your concerns, once and for all] on Him, for He cares for you affectionately and cares about you watchfully."*

Casting cares takes trust and humility. But that's the point. God wants you to trust His heart toward you. He wants you to know He loves you. He promises to take care of what concerns you, so put all that worries you into His almighty hands today!

A Prayer for Today

Dear Loving Father, thank You for making me wonderfully complete. I realize I've been prideful, trying to handle my problems on my own. I humbly cast all my cares, worries on You today. I leave my concerns in Your almighty hands. I am resting in you, it's Your problem now, not mine!

Day 38

Dependent-on-Daddy Child of God

Therefore whoever humbles himself as this little child
is the greatest in the kingdom of heaven.

—Matthew 18:4

Interestingly, Jesus refers to a child as humble. Think about it—what baby or young child can you think of that you would describe as *humble?* From the first cry, a baby is only concerned with himself. He doesn't care that his mother needs her sleep; he wants to be fed, wants to be dry, and wants to be held. His needs are utmost in his mind demanding an immediate response from the often weary parent! Babies are born self-centered. The parent's responsibility is to train this child to let go of selfishness and learn to be generous and kind and share with others.

So why would Jesus call this child *humble?* Jesus chose a child to illustrate the total dependency of the child on his parent. A child depends on his parents for food, a place to live, a warm bed at night, clothes, protection, wisdom, provision—basically for everything! A child never worries about paying the bills; he takes for granted that daddy's got that covered.

God's idea of humility is a complete dependence on Him, your Heavenly Father, for everything you need. That's why He put so many promises in His Word for you. He is a good, good Father and will take care of your needs when you trust Him (which takes humility) instead of trusting yourself and your plans (which Jesus calls pride.)

When God made the salvation plan to rescue you, it was not just so that your sins would be forgiven and you would go to heaven when you die. Instead, His desire is for you to live in His kingdom— experiencing His love and His Fatherly care for you, right here on earth!

Now, this does not mean that you sit back with your hands open, waiting for God to drop money in your lap. He tells us to work! But you can trust Him to provide employment, favor, and open doors of opportunity for you. By following God's written Word and listening to Holy Spirit's promptings, you will find yourself living in the abundant life He has planned for you.

A PRAYER FOR TODAY

Dear Heavenly Father: Your goodness and love for me are beyond measure! I let go of the reigns of my life. I choose to be humble and trust you for everything. I expect to see your provision and to experience your blessings beyond my wildest dreams!

Day 39

Triumphant Sword-Wielding Child of God

"There is no one like the God of Israel. He rides across the heavens to help you, across the skies in majestic splendor. The eternal God is your refuge, and his everlasting arms are under you. He drives out the enemy before you; he cries out, 'Destroy them! So Israel will live in safety, prosperous Jacob in security, in a land of grain and new wine, while the heavens drop down dew. How blessed you are, O Israel! Who else is like you, a people saved by the Lord? He is your protecting shield and your triumphant sword! Your enemies will cringe before you, and you will stomp on their backs!"

—Deuteronomy 33:26–29 NLT

I love sunrises. I find it breath-taking to witness the power of the sun exploding over the earth, destroying the darkness of the night. Starting with the first sliver of light and rising brighter and brighter until it completely dispels every sign of the darkness of the night just ended.

If worry, trauma, or fear have created tangible darkness in your soul, this promise of God's rescue is for you today. Just as the sun rises to dispel darkness—when you cry out to your Abba, Father, He comes to your rescue. Like the majestic power of the sun blasting across the night sky and lighting up the world, your Almighty Father will light up the dark places in your heart.

Galatians 3:29 says, *"And if you are Christ's, then you are Abraham's seed, and heirs according to the promise."* So where these verses refer to Israel and Jacob, you can personalize this promise for yourself.

"There is no one like the God of _____."

Put your name in there. Your God holds you in His almighty arms as He drives out your enemies.

If you're feeling depressed or fearful, your enemies are likely lying spirits or spirits of heaviness. God promises to be your protecting shield. But this scripture also says you need to take action, so God has given you an offensive weapon. *"Your triumphant sword!"* Your sword is the Word of God. Speak out loud God's promises to you, command the enemy to flee, lying spirits to go, in Jesus' name.

When you take action, look what this Word promises: *"Your enemies will cringe before you, and you will stomp on their backs!"* And the darkness in your life will disappear into His light.

A Prayer for Today

Father God, I would feel weak and hopeless if it weren't for Your amazing promises to me! You are my only hope. You have defeated my enemies, and I enforce that victory with your Word today. Thank you for coming to my rescue!

Day 40

ROYAL CHILD OF GOD

To Him who loved us and washed us from our sins in His own blood, and has made us kings and priests to His God and Father, to Him be glory and dominion forever and ever. Amen.

—Revelation 1:5–6

Decorating for Christmas is a four-day project at our house. I love transforming our home into a forest of evergreens with sparkling lights and bows and candles. I find unique little nooks to display my ever-growing accumulation of nativities and Christmas moose. The one-of-a-kind, made-with-love Saint Nicholas from my friend Kathy gets a special place of honor.

But of all my decorations, what heralds the true meaning of Christmas the loudest is the gold-and-white ribbon on our nine-foot-high living room tree. The ribbon boasts many of the names of Jesus: Savior, King of kings, Prince of Peace, Lamb of God, Bread of Life, Emmanuel, God with Us. The tree is topped with a golden crown, honoring the King of kings.

Have you ever wondered who are the "kings" over which Jesus is "King of kings"?

It's you and me—the children of God. We have been *made* kings!

It tells us in Revelation 1:5 that Jesus made us to be kings and priests to Him. As kings, we are to take dominion and reign in this world (Genesis 1:26).

Romans 5:17 (AMPC) says we are to live and reign as kings in this life. *"For if because of one man's trespass (lapse, offense) death reigned through that one, much more surely will those who receive [God's] overflowing grace (unmerited favor) and the free gift of righteousness [putting them into right standing with Himself] reign as kings in life through the one Man Jesus Christ (the Messiah, the Anointed One)."*

Kings enforce the borders of their kingdom. Kings take possession of their inheritance and enforce the victory over their enemies. Kings don't let the enemy run all over them, their family, their city, their nation, or anything that concerns them.

Kings don't just scrape by; they don't lack for anything they need. Kings are blessed and prosperous.

God wants you to take full advantage of all that Jesus came to earth to redeem for you. It gives Him glory when you take advantage of the superabundance He has for you. How do you do that? By claiming the promises that belong to you from His Word.

So whether you are reading this in July or December, King Jesus intends for you to reign as king on this earth. Don't shirk your duties or relinquish your authority to the enemy. Make your royal decrees according to God's Word. Stand firm and enforce God's Word and God's kingdom here on earth!

A Prayer for Today

Dear Father, I bow my knee to King Jesus today. You are the King of my life. I pray that You would give me a greater revelation of the authority You've given me to rule and reign on earth as Your representative.

Day 41

STEPPING-OUT-IN-POWER CHILD OF GOD

Every place that the sole of your foot will tread upon I have given you, as I said to Moses.

—Joshua 1:3

Recently I had terrible pain in the bottom of my foot. I was believing God for healing to manifest in my foot and the pain to leave. But I also did what I knew to do in the natural. I went to see my chiropractor.

As Dr. Ric was adjusting the bones in my foot, he told me something fascinating. He explained that the bottom of our foot has two bones that cross in the middle and then a little bone on top of that, which in medical term is called the cuboid or cornerstone bone. If that top cornerstone bone gets out of place, it can cause pain in the foot.

How awesome is that? Talk about being "fearfully and wonderfully made"! When God created you, He embedded the symbol of the cross and Jesus, your Cornerstone, in the bottom of your feet.

So literally, everywhere you go, you take the Gospel with you!

This bit of *anatomical revelation* also gives a deeper meaning to the fact that as a child of God, you can stomp your foot on the devil. The enemy is under your feet. Jesus and the cross crushed him!

So wherever you go today, you can be assured from the bottom of your feet on up that as a child of God, Jesus goes with you, and you have the victory.

Joshua continues to write in Joshua 1:9 (AMP): *"Have I not commanded you? Be strong and courageous! Do not be terrified or dismayed (intimidated), for the Lord your God is with you wherever you go."*

A Prayer for Today

Dear Heavenly Father, knowing that You put a symbol of Jesus and the cross in the bottom of my feet amazes me. Thank You for another reminder that everywhere I go, I take the Gospel with me. Help me to be bold and courageous to share Your love and claim my victory over the enemy with every step I take.

Day 42

CONFIDENT CHILD OF GOD

*And this is the confidence (the assurance, the privilege of boldness)
which we have in Him: [we are sure] that if we ask anything
(make any request) according to His will (in agreement with
His own plan), He listens to and hears us. And if (since) we
[positively] know that He listens to us in whatever we ask, we
also know [with settled and absolute knowledge] that we have
[granted us as our present possessions] the requests made of Him.*

—1 John 5:14–15 (AMP)

Our verse for today is one of my favorite foundational promises
in the whole Bible. But you might read it and think, *Yea, that's
great, but there's a catch. How do you know if you are praying "according
to His will"?*

I used to think that meant I had to end every prayer with the
caveat "if it be thy will." But praise God, I learned that you can pray
with confidence, knowing exactly what is God's will.

Here's the exciting truth: the Word of God is His will! You can
take any promise given in His Word (especially in the New Testament)
and apply it to your situation. God doesn't have a favorite son or
daughter who gets more than the other kids in the family. Any child
of God who grabs on to the promise by faith can have what it says!

For example, if you've been working for your boss "with excellence" as instructed in Colossians 3:23, but you are concerned about losing your position or being laid off, you need favor. So you can confidently claim the promise in Psalm 5:12. *"For You, O Lord, will bless the righteous; with favor, You will surround him as with a shield."* Then stand in faith knowing God has heard your prayer, according to today's verse, and that you have *"granted to you as your present possession the request you made of Him."* Then, rest in His promise and don't worry!

So what do you need today? wisdom, peace, provision, direction, safety, restoration, healing? These are all His will for you. Do you need some promises to claim? See the appendix for "70 Promises for an Abundant Life."

You can be confident in this—God hears you when you pray His Word and grants your request!

A Prayer for Today

Father, I love your Word! It is truth and life. No more guessing. Your Word shows me plainly Your will for my life. You are my loving Father who wants me blessed and living in abundance!

Day 43

DADDY'S CHILD

And because we are his children, God has sent the Spirit of his Son into our hearts, prompting us to call out, "Abba, Father."

—Galatians 4:6 (TNL)

When you received Jesus Christ as your Savior and Lord (Romans 10:10), you became a child of God. You also became a new creation. However, as you probably noticed, your body didn't change; your feelings didn't change, so what changed?

The Spirit of God came alive on the inside of you.

You could say you got a "Spirit transplant." You were *made* righteous and accepted by God through Jesus Christ, and God sent the Spirit of His Son into your heart. Now He desires that you know Him intimately as your Father, your Daddy, God.

People who have grown up in very traditional or formal churches get offended when I refer to Holy Father, Almighty God, as Daddy. But a Daddy relationship is precisely the kind of close, open, comfortable, loving family relationship your Father desires to have with you.

Abba is an Aramaic word used by small children when informally addressing their fathers. What name do most small children use in our society? Daddy.

So today, I want to encourage you to run into your Daddy's arms, sit on His lap, and share with Him your deepest desires, thoughts, and cares. Ask Him anything using Jesus' name as your power of attorney (John 14:13) and expect Him to answer you! He is your Father. He loves to give good gifts to His children.

"If you, imperfect as you are, know how to lovingly take care of your children and give them what's best, how much more ready is your heavenly Father to give wonderful gifts to those who ask him?" (Matthew 7:11 TPT).

A PRAYER FOR TODAY

Daddy God, I love you! You are a good, good Father, and I rest in Your love for me today.

Day 44

HOLY, FLAWLESS, RESTORED
CHILD OF GOD

Even though you were once distant from him, living in the shadows of your evil thoughts and actions, he reconnected you back to himself. He released his supernatural peace to you through the sacrifice of his own body as the sin-payment on your behalf so that you would dwell in his presence. And now there is nothing between you and Father God, for he sees you as holy, flawless, and restored, if indeed you continue to advance in faith, assured of a firm foundation to grow upon.

—Colossians 1:21–23a (TPT)

This scripture makes my jaw drop in amazement. Take some time to meditate on it. Let it sink into your spirit, especially the phrase *"And now there is nothing between you and Father God, for He sees you as holy, flawless, and restored."*

Jesus alone makes this status with God possible. His blood shed at the cross on your behalf made you righteous, made you holy, and restored you to full acceptance with your Heavenly Father. This is the good news of the Gospel!

Your part is to believe it, receive His gift, and trust in Him. That's what makes you a child of God.

This is the message I was privileged to share with young men, ages 15–25, at a drug and alcohol rehab center in Ecuador. The enemy had stolen their identity, deceived them into thinking they needed drugs or alcohol to "be somebody" when what they really needed was to see their true identity, to see themselves the way their Heavenly Father sees them—through Jesus—as holy, flawless, and restored.

When you understand your true identity in Jesus Christ, it will change the way you think. It will change the way you pray, it will change the way you speak, it will change the way you act. It will change your destiny.

But stay on guard. The enemy will constantly try to get you to doubt your identity, bring up your past mistakes, suggest you haven't read the Bible enough, prayed long enough, given enough, or served sufficiently to qualify for God's acceptance.

This truth of your identity in Christ is critical for you to remember as the last line of this scripture admonishes: *"If indeed you continue to advance in faith, assured of a firm foundation to grow upon."* With the truth that *"there is nothing between you and Father God, for He sees you as holy, flawless, and restored"* as your firm foundation, you can confidently jump up on Daddy's lap to ask and receive all the grace and mercy you need for today.

A Prayer for Today

Thank You, Father, that You see me as holy, flawless, and restored. This is too wonderful for me to comprehend. I know it is all because of Jesus. I accept His gift on my behalf. I rest in Your grace for me. Nothing that I do can make You love or accept me any more than You already do!

Day 45

PASSIONATELY PURSUED CHILD OF GOD

The Son of Man has come to give life to anyone who is lost. Think of it this way: If a man owns a hundred sheep and one lamb wanders away and is lost, won't he leave the ninety-nine grazing on the hillside and go out and thoroughly search for the one lost lamb? And if he finds his lost lamb, he rejoices over it, more than over the ninety-nine who are safe.

—Matthew 18:11–13 (TPT)

I love the fact that God pursues the lost lamb. When we are lost, His love comes looking for us.

When I was in Ecuador, God used me to bring back one of His lost lambs.

Before we left on our missions trip, we were instructed to leave any diamond rings at home. So that my hands wouldn't feel bare without my rings, I found a little mother-of-pearl ring with a cross on the top and a Bible verse inscription that read, "I can do all things through Christ who strengthens me." I decided it was perfect for our trip.

I wore the ring, but I had a feeling God had someone special in mind that He wanted me to give this ring to while I was in Ecuador. As I ministered to lots of ladies, I kept asking the Lord, *"Is this the one?"*

I was honored to be asked to bring the Sunday morning sermon at our host pastor's church. A word of knowledge was given following the sermon that there was someone who was struggling with deep depression and that God wanted to set them free that morning.

A young lady came up to me for prayer. I could tell she was very depressed. She had a heaviness and darkness about her that was almost tangible. I prayed for her and commanded the spirit of depression to leave and the joy of the Lord to flood her spirit. When we finished praying, I knew in my spirit that the ring was for her.

As I put the ring on her finger, I told Maria, "Your Father God wants you to know that this ring is a gift from Him. He sent me all the way from Colorado to give this ring to you. Every time you look at it, let it remind you that God loves you and is always right here with you."

The ring fit her finger perfectly. God even knew her ring size!

Her countenance lifted and Jesus' joy permeated her spirit. She was set free from the depression instantly!

God loved this young lady so much that He sent me to deliver a gift to her, straight from the heart of the Father! How thrilling for me to have the privilege of being His messenger.

God knows where you are today too. He knows where your lost child is or your wayward friend. Matthew 18:11–13 tells us that He'll leave the ninety-nine to pursue the lost sheep in your family, not to scold or punish but to show how much He cares and loves them.

He loves you that much.

A Prayer for Today

Dear Heavenly Father, in my mind, I know that You love me, but it's time we go deeper. I am not satisfied with a shallow acquaintance. I need a greater revelation of Your unconditional love for me and for those I love too. I want to know You more intimately. Let's spend more time together!

Day 46

More-Than-a-Conqueror Child of God

Yet in all these things we are more than conquerors through Him who loved us.

—Romans 8:37

For some reason, this verse in Romans always reminds me of the Super Bowl. The apostle Paul says Jesus made us "more than conquerors."

Did I mention I love football? It's a sad time for my husband and me when the center snaps the final play of the Super Bowl each February. Regardless of the champion, it means no more football for seven months!

My family is originally from Maine, and I was born in Boston, so I am inclined to be a New England Patriots fan. Tom Brady was the quarterback for many years. He won six Super Bowls and has been the MVP in five. He has earned over $196 million in his pro career.

However, who do you think is the *real* winner? His wife, Gisele.

She doesn't have to suit up, endure grueling daily practices, come home with bruises, sore muscles, or broken bones, but yet she gets to enjoy all the benefits of Tom's victorious career, private jet, huge mansion, and his big paycheck. She is "more than a conqueror!"

Way beyond football, Jesus is our champion. Jesus fought every battle for us, laid down His life willingly on the cross, broke all the curses and overcame the enemy on our behalf, and took back the keys to the kingdom for us. He did the work, yet we get all the benefits! He was made poor that we would be made rich!

Jesus made us *more* than conquerors! So whatever you need today, you can be confident in this promise too:

> *He who did not spare His own Son, but delivered Him up for us all, how shall He not with Him also freely give us all things? (Romans 8:32)*

A Prayer for Today

> *Thank You, Jesus, for laying down Your life, defeating the enemy, and breaking every curse. Because You rose again, I have victory in You, and nothing will defeat me. I trust in You. You are my hero!*

Day 47

THRILLING CHILD OF GOD

My dearest one, let me tell you how I see you—you are so thrilling
to me. To gaze upon you is like looking at one of Pharaoh's
finest horses—a strong, regal steed pulling his royal chariot.

—Song of Solomon 1:9 (TPT)

Song of Solomon is an often overlooked little book in the Old Testament. But there are some beautiful revelations of God's love and our value hidden in this romantic love letter. It is the story about the Shulamite woman and her Shepherd-King, Jesus. The first chapter begins with the Shulamite woman admitting she is "*so unworthy and in need.*" She goes on to describe her feelings as "*dark and dry as desert tents of the wandering nomads.*"

I can relate to feeling "dark and dry." Can you?

But look at how the Shepherd-King Jesus answers her in the next two verses:

> *Your tender cheeks are aglow—your earrings and gem-laden necklaces set them ablaze. We will enhance your beauty, encircling you with our golden reins of love. You will be marked with our redeeming grace. (Song of Solomon 1:10–11)*

"We" in verse eleven refers to the Trinity. Father, Son, and Holy Spirit are involved in making every Shulamite—every child of God—holy and radiant.

Think of it—God's love pouring out on your behalf, making you beautiful, making you righteous, making you worthy.

There is nothing you can do to add to your redemption—it is your free "beauty make-over from Jesus!" King Jesus did it all. He marked you with His redeeming grace. It is His grace alone that enhances your beauty.

Jesus plus *nothing* equals *everything*. That is the formula for grace. It is not about you working hard to be worthy. It is all about Jesus who *made* you worthy.

Meditate on this truth today: *You are thrilling to your King!*

A Prayer for Today

Father, the revelation of Your love continues to overwhelm me. I am worthy. I am valuable. I am beautiful. I am righteous, all because of Jesus. Thank You for Your redeeming grace!

Day 48

Predestined Child of God

For whom He foreknew, He also predestined to be conformed to the image of His Son, that He might be the firstborn among many brethren. Moreover whom He predestined, these He also called; whom He called, these He also justified; and whom He justified, these He also glorified.

—Romans 8:29–30

There is a lot of misunderstanding about predestination. Some people think it means God chose only certain people to be saved, and the rest are lost and doomed for hell.

When I learned the true meaning of this scripture, it blessed my socks off. So hold on to yours! God knows everything. So He has foreknowledge. This means that before He created the world, He could look into the future and see who would receive Jesus as their Savior and who would not.

Since He foreknew those who would choose to become part of His family, He made a plan for their life! Psalm 139:16 says, *"Your eyes saw my substance, being yet unformed. And in Your book they all were written, the days fashioned for me when as yet there were none of them."*

He wrote down His plan for your life before He even started creating the universe. He knew your name and wrote down a plan *for good and not evil;* it tells us in Jeremiah 29:11.

He prepared beforehand your destiny and purpose. Then He gave you the gifts and precursors for the skills you would need to accomplish your destiny. He went a step farther and included stocking the earth with all the provisions you would need to achieve that destiny.

Even the best of parents don't make these kinds of plans for their kids. But your perfect, loving Heavenly Father does! His meticulous planning demonstrates His over-the-top love for you. Never doubt that God loves you. He is on your side. He is cheering you on to accomplish your destiny.

A Prayer for Today

Father, You get the Best Father of All Eternity award! Thank You for showing me Your love by predestining and preparing for my life. Your ways are the best. I choose to follow close to You every day so that I will discover all You've written down for me—Your good plans, purpose, and destiny for my life.

Day 49

FAVORITE CHILD OF GOD

Keep me as the apple of your eye; hide me in the shadow of Your wings.

—Psalm 17:8

Yes, it's true; as a child of God—one who has received Jesus' gift of salvation and joined God's family—you are God's favorite. But wait, I'm God's favorite too. And the disciple John also stated he was God's favorite.

God says the earth is His footstool, so apparently, God is big enough to handle more than one favorite child!

Zechariah 2:8 says, *"For he who touches you, touches the apple of God's eye."*

To be "the apple of someone's eye" means to be their "favorite," the cherished object of their affections, to be regarded as incredibly precious and dear to them.

The apple of the eye is the center, the pupil. The word *pupil* comes from the Latin *pupilla*, meaning "little doll," referring to the tiny reflection one sees of oneself when looking into another person's eyes.

So think of this. God says that you are His favorite; you are most precious and dear to Him, the center of His attention. When He looks into your eyes, He sees the reflection of Jesus in you. It is because of Jesus that you are made righteous and accepted by the Father. Jesus is His beloved Son, and He sees Jesus in you!

If you are the apple of His eye, this also means you are never out of His sight. He is always watching over you, so you are never alone. Oh, dear child, you are indeed surrounded with *love*.

Regardless of what others say about you, your Creator God's opinion trumps all others—and He has eyes only for you!

A Prayer for Today

Dear Daddy God, I feel so special today, knowing that You love me best of all! Because I'm Your favorite, I know there is no good thing You will withhold from me. I am resting in Your unconditional love for me today.

Day 50

LOADED-DOWN-WITH-BENEFITS CHILD OF GOD

Blessed be the Lord, who daily loads us with
benefits, the God of our salvation!

—Psalm 68:19

I love early mornings. As the first glimmer of light peaks over the horizon, I love to shout, "Thank You, Lord, for another load of benefits!"

Maybe you're not an early riser, but whenever you get out of bed, I encourage you to look out your window and imagine a dump truck backing up in front of your house with a fresh load of benefits, a special delivery, just for you—wisdom, favor, healing, joy, goodness, strength, forgiveness, guidance, confidence, deliverance, protection, and peace!

God loves to give good gifts to His children. He loves it when we believe in Him and depend on Him. So whatever you need today, reach out, by faith and take it. Say, "Lord, I need wisdom today. I believe Your Word that says You will give me wisdom when I ask You for it."

Do you need provision? Then accept God's promise in Deuteronomy 8:18 and say, "Thank You, Lord, that You give me the power to get wealth. Thank You that because I am a tither, and I honor the Lord with my possessions, my vines will not stop bearing fruit, and all I do will prosper. I am a giver. The seed I have sown came from You, and I expect a great harvest" (2 Corinthians 9:10)!

Do you need healing? Then grab on tight to the benefit of healing that is promised to every child of God, saying, "Bless the Lord. I will not forget these benefits. You forgive all my iniquities, and you heal all my diseases" (Psalm 103:2–3)!

God has what you need. He is a good, good Father. Believe Him; trust His Word. If you need a promise to stand on today, see the appendix of this book for my list of "70 Promises for Abundant Life."

A Prayer for Today

Thank You, Father, that I don't have to struggle through this day on my own. You are eager to help me. You are always faithful to keep your promises to me, so I accept by faith precisely what I need for today. Thank you for another dump truck full of benefits!

Day 51

EARTH-KING CHILD OF GOD

Our Father in heaven, hallowed be Your name. Your kingdom
come. Your will be done on earth as it is in heaven.

—Matthew 6:9–10

This may shock you, but one of the most dangerous but common statements made in Christian circles today is this: "God is in control." This seems to be the standard explanation to comfort one's self in a situation that makes no sense. I'm sure you've heard people say, "Well, I'm sure glad God is in control!" Maybe you've even said it yourself. Songs have even been written proclaiming it. My response to this effort of spirituality is, *if God's in control, He's sure not doing a very good job!*

Surprisingly, you won't find the phrase "God is in control" anywhere in the Bible. What you will find is that God gave us dominion over all the earth.

In Genesis 1:26, *God said, "Let Us make man in Our image, according to Our likeness; let them have dominion…over all the earth."* (God may regret that He ever said that, but the Word says He never changes his mind or goes back on his word—so He's stuck with us!)

Psalm 8:4–6 says,

What is man that You are mindful of him, and the son of man that you visit him? For You have made him a little lower than Elohim, and You have crowned him with glory and honor. You have made him to have dominion over the works of Your hands; You have put all things under his feet.

And Psalm 15:16 clearly delineates the authority, *"The heaven, even the heavens are the Lord's; but the earth He has given to the children of men."*

No wonder why when Jesus taught his disciples to pray what we call the Lord's Prayer, the very first thing He told them to pray is *"Your kingdom come, Your will be done, on earth as it is in heaven"*!

Unless we give God authority to come and do His will on earth, we are on our own. God is a gentleman. He is a God of choice. He will not step into a situation where He is not invited.

If you're smart, you'll invite Him into every area of your life—every day! Declare to Almighty God, *"Your Kingdom come, and Your will be done"* in your family, your work, your finances, and especially in our nation today. God stands with arms wide open, offering His assistance, desperately wanting to help you today. The truth is, *you are in control.*

So if you want to give God the control in your life, tell Him! Pray the first prayer Jesus taught us to pray.

A PRAYER FOR TODAY

My Heavenly Father, I praise You and honor Your name. I declare Your kingdom come. Your will be done—in my family, my marriage, my church, and in America—just as it is in heaven.

Day 52

HEAVEN-DECLARING CHILD OF GOD

I will give you the keys of heaven's kingdom realm to forbid on earth that which is forbidden in heaven, and to release on earth that which is released in heaven.

—Matthew 16:19 (TPT)

Yesterday, I may have tipped over a sacred cow with my bold announcement that you are in control in this earth, not God. I'd like to expound on that—before you throw this book at me!

God is sovereign. He is overall. He created everything and set boundaries for the earth, seas, sun, and moon and ordained the world's end and future judgment and rewards.

However, the Sovereign One is also a God of choice. He desires free-will relationships. He gives us an option to choose Him and join His family or reject Him. We are not puppets in His hand that He moves on a whim whichever way He chooses. He doesn't pick some to be His children, while others are left out. The sovereign doctrine says that we have no say in the matter, and everything that happens in this world is God's will. The upside to believing this way is that it takes all the pressure and responsibility off us.

But in Matthew 16, Jesus is handing over the keys of His kingdom to the children of God with solemn instructions to *"forbid on earth that which is forbidden in heaven, and to release on earth that which is released in heaven."* This is another way of saying, "I'm putting you in charge here to declare and enforce 'His Kingdom come, His will be done on earth, as it is in heaven.'"

So you might be thinking, *How do I know what His will is for the earth?*

For all our answers, we look to Jesus. He said, *"For I have come down from heaven, not to do My own will, but the will of Him who sent Me"* (John 6:38).

So what did Jesus do on earth? At the start of His ministry, Jesus announced His purpose on earth,

> *God has anointed Me to preach the gospel to the poor; He has sent Me to heal the brokenhearted, to proclaim liberty to the captives and recovery of sight to the blind, to set at liberty those who are oppressed; and to proclaim [the day when salvation and the free favors of God profusely abound].* (Luke 4:18–19 AMP)

Bottom line, Jesus came to earth to redeem humanity, set right the wrongs, and defeat all the ways the devil has tried to destroy mankind.

That's where we come in! *Love has been perfected among us in this…because as He is, so are we in this world* (1 John 4:17).

So here's how that looks practically. As you watch the evening news, hear of corruption in our government, see violence in our streets, weep at the injustice and horrors of child trafficking, mourn over the number of aborted babies, become aware of the scheme to promote the LBGT agenda in schools, or see another friend's marriage end in divorce, you take action. You stand up boldly, holding the keys to the kingdom, and pronounce God's peace, blessings, restoration, and glory.

Order the devil and demonic forces to take their hands off your family, schools, churches, and America. Take your authority and invite God's power to rule as you enforce God's will be done here on earth just like it is in heaven! Then go a step farther and ask God for wisdom and strategies to know your part in physically taking action to turn back the evil and bring light to the world.

A Prayer for Today

Heavenly Father, only with the Holy Spirit's strength, power, love, and wisdom can I assume the role You've entrusted to me here on earth. I dedicate myself to You. Use my mouth, my hands, and feet and give me strategies to enforce the authority You've given me so that You can rule and reign on earth through me. I declare Your Kingdom come, and Your will be done!

Day 53

WORRY-FREE CHILD OF GOD

*Don't worry about anything; instead, pray about everything. Tell God
what you need, and thank him for all he has done. Then you will
experience God's peace, which exceeds anything we can understand. His
peace will guard your hearts and minds as you live in Christ Jesus.*

—Philippians 4:6–7 (NLT)

When I was a young mother with small children, I used to say, "Of course, I worry. I'm a mother!"

But then I realized that God's Word says, *"Do not worry about anything."* God wouldn't tell us to do something impossible, right? So it must not only be possible but essential for us not to worry.

The book of Job tells us how dangerous worrying is. There is a lot of misunderstanding about Job. It is the oldest book in the Bible. Job had many false beliefs about God, which get straightened out in the last few chapters, but unfortunately, preachers have developed many false doctrines from the book of Job.

This may surprise you, but bottom line, what initiated Job's tragedies and loss was this: Job was worried about his kids.

Job's adult children liked to party, (to drink and feast together) so, in case they sinned, Job would regularly offer sacrifices on their behalf. Job 1:5 says, *"For Job said to himself, 'Perhaps my children have sinned and have cursed God in their hearts.'"* So as a hedge against his fear, *"making offering sacrifices for his kids was Job's regular practice."*

Fear and worry over his kids opened the door to the enemy.

In Job 1:12, God says to Satan, *"Behold all he has is in your power; only do not lay a hand on his life."* People have misinterpreted this to mean that God was permitting the devil to bring evil on Job. That's not true. God was merely observing that Job had opened the door to the enemy by worrying about his kids. Job was unknowingly allowing Satan to wreak havoc in his life.

Worry, which is sin, is what allows the devil access to you. That's a dangerous place to be.

So you have a choice you make: worry or trust God. Replace your worry thoughts with *Word* thoughts. Here's a good thought to start with: "The God who created the universe, my Father, cares for me personally!"

When you pray and thank God for what He's done for you and His care over you, then Philippians 4:7 promises you God's peace even in trials.

At the end of the book of Job, he finally realizes the truth about God and identifies the enemy as the source of his loss, then God was able to restore Job and give him double for all his trouble!

Check out "70 Promises for an Abundant Life" in the appendix. There are some powerful promises you can claim to make your day worry-free.

A Prayer for Today

Heavenly Father, thank You for loving me so much that You don't want me to worry about anything. I shut the door to the enemy, and I choose to rest in Your promises and trust You today, no matter how impossible it looks to me in the natural. You are my Supernatural, Miracle-working, Promise-keeping, Dad!

Day 54

WISER-THAN-JOB CHILD OF GOD

*Therefore, I have uttered what I did not understand, things
too wonderful for me, which I did not know... I have heard
of You by the hearing of the ear, but now my eye sees You.
Therefore, I abhor myself, and repent in dust and ashes.*

—Job 42:5–6

What did Job utter that he did not understand? *Plenty!*

Since I brought up Job in yesterday's devotional, I want
to take a few more days to give some perspective on the book of Job.

More false theologies and misunderstandings about God's character come from the book of Job than any other book in the Bible.

Here's the one that rubs me the worst.

There is a popular chorus that contains the phrase "you give
and take away, my heart will choose to say, blessed be the name of the
Lord." This phrase is found in Job 1:21:

*"Naked I came from my mother's womb, and naked
I will depart. The Lord gave, and the Lord has taken
away; may the name of the Lord be praised."*

Is it true that the Lord gives and the Lord takes away? It's generally accepted to be that way. But that is a totally false accusation against God. Unfortunately, singing any doctrine often enough, we start to believe it without questioning its accuracy.

Most people today respond to tragedy the same way Job did—they blame God. Insurance companies even label natural disasters as "acts of God." I heard an eyewitness being interviewed by a news reporter on the scene after a tragic accident that took the life of a two-year-old say, "We don't understand why God would take this child."

But did God take the child?

In John 10:10, Jesus clearly tells us that Satan's sole purpose is to steal, kill and destroy. He thrives on tragedy and disasters in this world.

As I've mentioned, the book of Job is the oldest in the Bible. Job lived before Abraham and had very little understanding of God. He also did not know that we have an enemy in this world—Satan.

We can learn a wealth of information about what life was like during Job's era and interesting facts about animals, but don't take your theology from this book!

At the end of the book, after an encounter with God, Job actually retracts what he said earlier about God giving and taking away when Job confesses, "I uttered what I did not know, I repent!"

Here's why it is so crucial for you to know this truth.

If you think God gives and takes away, then you will play right into Satan's hand. He wants to steal your health, your finances, and your life. But if you think God is taking it from you, perhaps to teach you a lesson, then you won't stand up and demand what God has promised to you as His child, especially when it concerns healing.

You can know for sure that God is on your side. He promises you healing, provision, restoration, protection, and wisdom. Take what belongs to you and don't let the enemy convince you that God took it from you. God is good all the time!

A Prayer for Today

Dear Heavenly Father, like Job I realize I've had a false concept of Your loving character and have not trusted

You completely. Show me where I've misunderstood You. Teach me to embrace the truth so that I can fully accept all You desire for me as Your child.

Day 55

PRIVILEGED-WITH-TRUTH CHILD OF GOD

For I am the Lord, I do not change.

—Malachi 3:6a

Job was the richest man of his day. He knew that God created the world, and he attributed his wealth to God. (The absurd idea of evolution hadn't occurred to him.) He worshipped God even though he was ignorant of God's true character.

What Job did not know was that his predecessors, Adam and Eve, had disobeyed God and given over their dominion of the earth to the devil. The god of this world was out to get Job because he despised Job's worship of God.

Job ignorantly attributed everything, both good and bad, as coming from God. When his wife coldly suggested that he "curse God and die," Job responded, *"Shall we indeed accept good from God, and shall we not accept adversity?"* (Job 2:9).

If you study the book of Job, you will find seventy-four times that Job falsely accused God! Here are just four of Job's accusations:

- God has delivered me to the ungodly.
- God is not just.

- God doesn't hear me.
- God counts me as one of his enemies (Job 16:11–14, 19:7–11)

The devil has no new tricks. He still tries every day to get us to believe lies about God. That's why you've got to keep reminding yourself of the truth of the Word of God. Otherwise, you'll be tricked into accusing God too.

Unlike Job, we are privileged to have the whole Word of God. We have all His truths and promises and can see God's true nature for ourselves.

Job needed to hear these truths from God's Word:

> But the Lord is faithful, and he will strengthen you and protect you from the evil one. (2 Thessalonians 3:3)

> For I, the Lord, love justice. (Isaiah 61:8a)

> For the eyes of the Lord are on the righteous, and his ears are attentive to their prayer, but the face of the Lord is against those who do evil. (1 Peter 3:12)

> I no longer call you servants because a servant does not know his master's business. Instead, I have called you friends, for everything that I learned from my Father I have made known to you. (John 15:15)

As you go throughout your day, remember that you are a privileged and favored child of God. God is good, and the devil is bad. The enemy has no right to steal from you, so stand your ground against him.

A Prayer for Today

> Heavenly Father, I am so thankful that You allowed me to be born in this generation and not in Job's time.

Thank You for preserving the Bible over two thousand years so that I can know You, Your ways, and Your goodness to me. I love You, Lord.

Day 56

Born-Again Child of God

By his divine power, God has given us everything we need for living a godly life. We have received all of this by coming to know him, the one who called us to himself by means of his marvelous glory and excellence. And because of his beauty and excellence, he has given us great and precious promises. These are the promises that enable you to share his divine nature and escape the world's corruption caused by human desires.

—2 Peter 1:3–4 (NLT)

There are many reasons you should not draw any conclusions about God's character toward His kids from the book of Job—here are two more important reasons.

First of all, Job was not born-again.

When you believe in Jesus Christ and what He accomplished for you at the cross, the Bible says you are born again (Romans 10:9). That salvation includes covenant protection, provision, healing, forgiveness, safety, and restoration. Jesus Christ has transported you from the kingdom of darkness into the kingdom of God (Colossians 1:13).

If you've not been appropriating your full "salvation benefits package," now is an excellent time to start. Tell God that from now on, you are claiming what belongs to you as His child!

Secondly, Job did not have the spiritual weapons to stand against the devil's attacks like you do.

This reminds me of a very negative woman I know. When I would ask her "how are you?" she'd respond, "Oh, the devil has really been attacking me lately." To which, I would respond, "Don't let him get away with that!"

As a child of God, you have dominion over the devil.

In James 4:7 in the Passion Translation, Paul tells us how to fight the devil, *"So then, surrender to God. Stand up to the devil and resist him, and he will turn and run away from you."*

So unlike Job, you have the power inside you to stand up to every attack that comes against you.

If you read the book of Job, it seems his troubles go on forever. But actually, they lasted about nine months.

When Job finally realized that God was good all the time and was not the one who brought loss and tragedy on him and his family, he changed his tune! As soon as he did, God demonstrated His true character to Job by doubly restoring all that Job had lost.

It says in Job 42:12, *"So the Lord blessed Job in the second half of his life even more than in the beginning. For now, he had 14,000 sheep, 6,000 camels, 1,000 teams of oxen, and 1,000 female donkeys. He also gave Job seven more sons and three more daughters."*

So here's what I hope you've learned from these last few days focusing on Job: God is good all the time. Job was ignorant of the truths that you know today as a child of God. It's not true that God gives and takes away.

God gives and gives and gives because He loves and loves and loves you—more than you can imagine!

A Prayer for Today

Father, thank You that as Your child, I have all the benefits and promises of salvation. Thank You for showing me that I have authority over the devil. I submit to You, and he must flee. In areas of my life where the devil has stolen from me, I expect that You will restore double to me.

Day 57

FEARLESS CHILD OF GOD

There is no fear in love; but perfect love casts out fear.

—1 John 4:18

Children are fearless.

When my children were little, they thought nothing of flinging themselves off the top of the jungle gym into their daddy's waiting arms. It never crossed their mind that he might drop them! They didn't worry about food to eat, a bed to sleep in, clothes to wear, or how to pay their college tuition. They never gave it a thought.

They trusted their father to provide for them and protect them, they had no reason to fear because they knew their father's love. Knowing Father God's love and believing what He has said is faith. Faith pleases God (Hebrews 11:6).

I admit there are plenty of reasons to be fearful in our world today. But even amid government tyranny, riots, open borders, human trafficking, and devastating storms wreaking havoc, God says, "Fear not." How is that possible?

God hates fear. Fear empowers the enemy and hinders you from your destiny and from receiving all God's promises meant for you. That's why every time Jesus or His angel messengers felt fear rise up in someone, the first thing they said to them was, "Fear not." Although

I've not counted them myself, I'm told that the warning "fear not" appears 365 times in the Bible, one for every day of the year.

God planned your arrival on earth to coincide with this critical time in history, when Christ's return appears imminent! He equipped you with strategic skills and gifts designed for your world-impacting assignment, a job meant to be accomplished only in partnership with Him. A great harvest is sweeping our world, and laborers are needed!

Perhaps your assignment is to share the gospel with a neighbor, speak up at the school board meeting to oppose critical race ctheory, or run for a public office to help bring righteous rule back to our nation. You may be tempted to shrink back in fear and think *No way*, but your Heavenly Father is saying, "Take a leap of faith! Jump to Me! I'll catch you. Trust My love. I won't let you fall."

The song "No Longer Slaves" by Bethel Music powerfully declares the child of God's freedom from fear through God's perfect love:

> I'm no longer a slave to fear. I am a child of God
> From my mother's womb, You have chosen me
> Love has called my name.
> I've been born again into a family.
> Your blood flows through my veins.
> You split the sea
> So I could walk right through it
> My fears are drowned in perfect love
> You rescued me
> And I will stand and sing
> I am a child of God

As the song says, there is no longer a reason to fear when you know how much your Heavenly Father loves you. When you feel fear, catch yourself and find a promise from your Father and claim it in faith! Daddy's got you. Together, you can accomplish the impossible!

A Prayer for Today

Faithful, loving Father, You demonstrated your unfailing, unconditional love for me at the cross; so I know you will never let me down now. I let go of fear and step out in faith and boldness surrounded by Your love. I know with You and I working in partnership, there's nothing we cannot do!

Day 58

GENUINE CHILD OF GOD

And you shall know the truth, and the truth shall make you free.

—John 8:32

B elieving lies can have devastating consequences in your life.
I am tenacious about sharing truth. I want you to know your true identity as a child of God. And I am also passionate about helping you understand and grasp the covenant inheritance that belongs to you in God's family!

Everywhere we look, the enemy is trying to steal identity. It's so bad in our world today that some people don't even know which public bathroom to use! This is one of the cruelest lies of the enemy.

When you don't know who you are and don't realize what belongs to you as a child of God, it is easy for the enemy to steal, kill, and destroy—which is precisely his plan for your life (John 10:10).

I used to work as a bank teller, and I had to learn how to identify counterfeit one-hundred-dollar bills. Rather than studying an assortment of fake bills, I handled the real thing. After weeks and weeks of counting genuine hundred dollar bills, I became so familiar with the look and feel of the currency that I could easily spot a fake.

It works the same with spotting the lies the enemy throws at you. When you don't know the truth, it is easy to be deceived, get discouraged, and lose hope. If you are spending more time watching the mainstream news than reading your Bible, you are in a dangerous place.

Study the truth so you won't fall for the lies. Instead, you'll develop a discerning spirit and strength and wisdom to stand against the enemy's schemes in the world.

That's why it is essential to renew your mind every day on what God's Word says is true about *who* you are and *whose* you are.

These are just a few of the many truths about you found in God's Word*:

- *Even before the creation of the world, you were planned.*
- *God created male and female and blessed them.*
- *You are a child of the King, adopted into His family.*
- *An heir in Christ.*
- *Accepted in the Beloved.*
- *You were made righteous and accepted by God through Jesus Christ.*
- *You are blessed with every spiritual blessing in heavenly places.*
- *You lack no good thing.*
- *You have an abundance for every good work.*
- *God predestined you for success.*

You are special. So stand tall, be bold, and act like the King's child that you are through Jesus Christ!

A Prayer for Today

Holy Spirit teach me to discern the enemy's attempts of identity theft against me. Your word is truth. I am an heir of God and destined for success in Your kingdom!

---

* Ephesians 1:3–6, Romans 8:17, 2 Corinthians 5:17, Psalm 34:10, 2 Corinthians 9:8, Romans 8:28–30

Day 59

CARED-FOR CHILD OF GOD

Casting all your care upon Him, for He cares for you.

—1 Peter 5:7

I want to share with you a revelation that helped me to stop worrying and start casting. Worry is sin.

As a child of God, your Father says to you *"do not worry," period* (Philippians 4:6).

Did you know that the root cause of worry is *pride*?

When you don't trust God, and you try to handle your problems on your own, God calls that pride. Children seem to demonstrate this prideful independence at a very young age. You might think it's cute when a three-year-old refuses help zipping their jacket. "I can do it myself" they say as they stomp their feet in defiance of Mother's help, even though Mom can see clearly that the fabric is caught, and they'll never get it zipped without help. Sometimes we do the same thing with Father God.

First Peter 5:7 may have been a memory verse when you were young. But that is just the last half of the sentence. As Paul Harvey used to say, "Here's the rest of the story." The full sentence reads: *"Therefore humble yourselves under the mighty hand of God, that He may exalt you in due time, casting all your care upon Him, for He cares for you"* (1 Peter 5:6–7).

Humbling yourself means giving God your cares, worries, distractions, burdens, and anxieties. When you try to handle your problems on your own, you are saying to your Almighty Father God, "Take your hands off. I've got this!"

And the verse before that says, "God resists the proud, but gives grace to the humble." I am sure you don't want to be "resisted by God," especially when you have a problem. That's when you need Him most!

What a loving Father who insists that His kids not be burdened down with problems. Your Father is saying to you, "Let Daddy handle it."

So let Him!

A Prayer for Today

Father, You're serious. You don't want me to worry about a single thing! I can see now how trying to handle my problems on my own is pride. It's saying I can do it better than you. No way! I am asking for your help. I put my cares into Your capable and mighty hands. I expect You to handle my concerns as I trust in You.

Day 60

FAITH-AND-PATIENCE-MOVED CHILD OF GOD

So don't allow your hearts to grow dull or lose your enthusiasm, but follow the example of those who fully received what God has promised because of their strong faith and patient endurance.

—Hebrews 6:12 (TPT)

Begging God isn't pretty, and it's very unnecessary when it comes to receiving from God. He has already provided everything you need for life and godliness.

At the cross, Jesus broke every curse, redeemed you, set you free from condemnation, and has already blessed you along with faithful Abraham. Then Jesus said, *"It is finished."*

One of the Names of God is *Jehovah Jireh*, which means "God sees ahead and provides." It's like Jesus went to the store and already purchased everything you would need for your life to fulfill your purpose here on earth. He stockpiled your pantry shelves with all that you'll require. He provided for your healing, your financial provision, safety, protection, wisdom, and restoration.

So you may be thinking, *That's great. But how do I get the provision off the pantry shelf and into my hands?*

The answer is in Hebrews 6:12, *"Imitate those who through faith and patience inherit the promises."* It is by your faith that you inherit the promises. You start speaking and claiming what's yours! And you keep standing in faith with patience, not quitting, not throwing in the towel and giving up.

To inherit means *"to receive by virtue of being heir to it."* You are an heir of God. You receive all that He has promised by faith because it already belongs to you! Rather than moving *toward* getting healed, you speak from the position of *already having the victory*, already being healed—and enforcing that victory.

A PRAYER FOR TODAY

Heavenly Father, with a heart of faith in Jesus' finished work for me, I say thank You, Lord, that by the stripes of Jesus, I was healed at the cross, and so I am healed now. I declare that the same power that raised Jesus from the dead is alive in me. Thank You for loving me so much that You've provided everything I need. (1 Peter 2:24, Ephesians 1:19–20)

Day 61

VICTORIOUS CHILD OF THE LIVING GOD

If you confess with your mouth the Lord Jesus and believe in your heart that God has raised Him from the dead, you will be saved.

—Romans 10:9

By far, the most important holiday of the whole year is Easter or Resurrection Sunday. Some might argue that Christmas tops the list, but if Jesus hadn't risen from the dead, we would have nothing to celebrate—ever.

As a young child, I was taught the traditional Easter greeting that dates back to the days of Emperor Tiberius. The Catholic Church calls it the Paschal greeting. One would say, *"He is risen."* To which, you would reply, *"He is risen indeed!"*

I text "He is risen" to my kids early every Easter morning to make sure they still remember the correct response. I am happy to say they always pass my test!

Our entire salvation is dependent on Jesus' resurrection.

If Jesus is still dead, then we aren't forgiven. First Corinthians 15:16–17 says, *"For if the dead do not rise, then Christ is not risen. And if Christ is not risen, your faith is futile; you are still in your sins!"*

If He were still dead, then the price wasn't paid. The curses were not broken. We are still slaves to sin.

But He was raised!

As it says in Romans 10:9, to be saved, to become a child of God, you must not only confess Jesus Christ as Lord but also believe in the resurrection.

Life would have no meaning if there was no resurrection. But because He is alive, you have victory over everything the devil tries to throw your way.

The most powerful message of the Gospel is that Jesus is alive. He has risen! Because Jesus is alive, the devil is defeated. Because Jesus is alive, the power and curses of Satan over you and your family are forever broken, and you are released from the bondage of sin. Because Jesus is alive, your healing is assured. Because Jesus is alive, you are made righteous, and your relationship with Father God is restored.

You can't earn this salvation. Your part is to believe and receive all that Jesus' victory over death has purchased for you.

Every day is Resurrection Day—it's a Victory Day for every child of God.

A Prayer for Today

Dear Heavenly Father, Jesus Christ, Holy Spirit, thank You for Your great plan of redemption. You were all in on it together. If it weren't for Your great love for me, I would be lost for all eternity. Out of a heart of gratitude, I give myself to You today. I want to share this truth with everyone I meet—He is risen indeed!

Day 62

RESURRECTION POWERED
CHILD OF GOD

*I pray that you will continually experience the immeasurable
greatness of God's power made available to you through faith.
Then your lives will be an advertisement of this immense power as
it works through you! This is the mighty power that was released
when God raised Christ from the dead and exalted him to the place
of highest honor and supreme authority in the heavenly realm!*

—Ephesians 1:19–20 (TPT)

Think about this—the resurrection power that raised Jesus to life is in you!

God exerted His creation power when He spoke, "Let there be light." And there was light. When He said, "Let the earth bring forth the living creatures," and it was so. When God said, "Let Us make man in Our own image," He created them male and female. He is Almighty God, the Creator of the universe. But there was nothing recorded in scripture that opposed His creative power during the six days of creation.

On the other hand, the power it took to raise Jesus from the dead met with the opposition of every demon in hell! On the cross, Jesus took on Himself the sin and corruption of the whole world: every curse, every sickness, every deformity, every degeneration, every pain was put on His body. When He was laid in the tomb, Satan thought he'd won. But Colossians 2:15 tells us that Jesus *"disarmed principalities and powers, He made a public spectacle of them, triumphing over them in it."* Jesus' sinless, perfect, holy blood was poured out for us and defeated the law of sin and death (Romans 8:2). His resurrection power overcame every curse and every evil, diabolical scheme and force leveled against Him—and against you!

This is the same resurrection power that is in you—power to enforce the victory over the enemy that Jesus already won. The apostle Paul explains that the switch to flip on this resurrection power is your faith. Just believe!

This power breaks curses, destroys bondages, and uproots depression and guilt. It's the power that can take the mess in your life, or your neighbor's life, and resurrect it into something beautiful.

God is in the business of reviving and bringing life to impossible-looking situations. Nothing is too hard for Him.

He has ways to rescue your child, renovate your marriage, reconstruct your financial situation, or impact your neighborhood with His miraculous resurrection power. Listen to Him, follow His Word, and trust His power at work in you.

Expect God's resurrection power to explode like fireworks in your life today!

A Prayer for Today

Dear Victorious Lord Jesus, thank you for taking all my guilt, sin, sickness, and shame with you to the cross. It was buried with you there, and now, I am raised to new life and infused with your resurrection power! Let it flow out to others. Holy Spirit, teach me to wield this resurrection power. Enforce the victory Jesus won and share His life-giving love with others.

Day 63

LACKING NOTHING CHILD OF GOD

The Lord is my shepherd, I lack nothing.

—Psalm 23:1 (NIV)

David, the shepherd, with his firsthand experience of shepherding, expertly describes the life of sheep under the care of a good shepherd. The flock's health reflects the shepherd's love, expertise, diligence, care, and provision for his sheep. I want to make the Good Shepherd look good, don't you?

How can you make Jesus look good? By trusting Him, following His direction, resting in His goodness, and feeding on the good things He provides in His pastures.

A few years ago, I was diagnosed with AMD (age-related macular degeneration), hemorrhaging behind the macula in my left eye, which destroys the central vision.

After the diagnosis, I found myself continually focusing on my eyesight. One of AMD's symptoms is seeing wavy lines instead of straight lines. The nurse gave me an Amsler grid chart and told me to look at it every morning to test if my eyesight was getting worse.

I discovered something. I was focusing on my lack of clear eyesight.

But Psalm 23:1 says that *"I lack nothing."* So I decided to look at my Shepherd instead of the chart. I was determined to focus on my Healer and all His promises and not focus on my lack—the problem.

When I did this, an amazing thing happened—my eyesight improved! I still have some wiggly lines in my vision, but I hardly notice them anymore, and every day it is improving. I had a vision test and the doctor was amazed that now I can read the letters all the way across the eye chart, not just the letters down the left side. My Shepherd is my Healer!

What are you focusing on today?

Turn your focus from your inadequacies or lack to your almighty, loving Father—Jehovah Jireh, your Provider, and Jehovah Rapha, your Healer.

A Prayer for Today

Heavenly Father, You are the best Shepherd in the world! Thank You for Your constant care and provision. I do not want or lack. You are my source of everything I need. Today I choose to keep my focus on You. Thank You that Your goodness and love are pursuing me all day long.

Day 64

GRACE-INFUSED CHILD OF GOD

God's grace is sufficient for you.

—2 Corinthians 12:9

The word *grace* is used a lot in the Christian community for everything from singing "Amazing Grace" to saying grace before dinner.

So what exactly is this "amazing grace"?

Paul tells us in Ephesians 2:8, *"For by grace are you saved through faith."* At the cross, God did for us through Jesus' sacrifice what we could never do for ourselves. He saved us. This was God's grace in action! A popular acronym for GRACE is God's Riches at Christ's Expense. I used to think that was all there was to grace.

Fortunately for us, God's grace goes a lot further than that. God's grace was not a one-time event only demonstrated at the cross. His grace is our *power*. As a child of God, you are entitled to draw on God's grace every day of your life.

I like this definition of *grace* best: *God's grace is God's supernatural power at work on your behalf doing for you what you could never do for yourself.*

Think about it—on your own:

• Are you capable of being the parent your kids need?

- Having the wisdom to respond accurately in every situation?
- Making correct decisions all the time on your job?
- Responding with patience and love to your spouse consistently?
- Finding your car keys?
- Loving your neighbor as yourself?

If you're like me, I bet you're thinking "no way!" That's why you need God's grace!

Your Heavenly Father is patiently waiting to give you His *supernatural power boost* for the challenge you face today.

A Prayer for Today

Lord, I ask for and I receive Your grace for today.
Thank You that in every situation and every conversation,
You are empowering me with what I need to prosper.

Day 65

OH-SO-SPECIAL CHILD OF GOD

*Every single moment you are thinking of me! How precious and
wonderful to consider that you cherish me constantly in your every
thought! O God, your desires toward me are more than the grains of
sand on every shore! When I awake each morning, you're still with me.*

—Psalm 139:17–18 (TPT)

Do you realize how special you are to your Heavenly Father?

The apostle Paul prayed for us to get a revelation of just
how marvelous this truth is in Ephesians 1:18. He asked the Father
to show us *"what are the riches of the glory of His inheritance in the
saints."*

You are God's inheritance. He says having you as His child
makes Him rich!

If you are a parent, I am sure that you would agree that your
children are a treasure to you—most of the time anyway!

Well, that's how your Heavenly Father feels about you all the
time. As a child of God, you are a treasure to your Father. You make
Him rich and fulfilled.

The enemy likes to throw lies at you, telling you that you are
not valuable, you are not important, you are not worth much.

But God says just the opposite. You are so special to Him that He can't stop thinking about you. In Zephaniah 3:17, it says that *"He rejoices over you with shouts of joy and dancing!"*

Now if you are thinking, That sounds nice, but God couldn't possibly love me like that, remember His love is not based on how good you are but on how good Jesus is on your behalf. Jesus made you righteous. He put you in right standing with the Father through His death and resurrection (2 Corinthians 5:21).

Simply accept it! Your Heavenly Father is crazy about you. The mere mention of your name makes Him celebrate!

A Prayer for Today

Dear Father, I pray that You will open my eyes to see myself the way You see me—created in Your image, made righteous by the blood of Jesus and special to You!

Day 66

JESUS-WRAPPED CHILD OF GOD

Every spiritual blessing in the heavenly realm has already been
lavished upon us as a love gift from our wonderful heavenly Father,
the Father of our Lord Jesus—all because he sees us wrapped
into Christ. This is why we celebrate him with all our hearts!

—Ephesians 1:3 (TPT)

Because of Jesus' sacrifice for you on the cross and your belief and acceptance of His gift of salvation, you have been made righteous. There is no amount of human effort that can make you any more accepted by God than what Jesus has already made you.

When God looks at you, He sees Jesus' righteousness, holiness, and purity. If you think that your behavior will change God's view of you, then you're saying that your works are stronger than the blood of Jesus.

But in Ephesians 1:3, Paul says that God sees us *"wrapped into Christ."*

I have a pancake recipe that my grandkids request for breakfast almost every time they spend the night. I mix flour, cottage cheese, eggs, and vanilla in one bowl. Then I beat egg whites in another bowl and fold them into the batter. After I fold in the egg whites, it would be impossible to separate them from the mixture. They have been folded in. That's what we look like when we are wrapped into Christ.

We have become *one* with him. So when the Father says that He loves us as He loves Jesus (John 17:23), it's because in the Spirit, He can't tell us apart. We are one!

If this seems difficult to believe, ask the Lord to confirm His word to you. Colossians 1:27 tells us this is the mystery of the gospel, *"To them, God willed to make known what are the riches of the glory of this mystery among the Gentiles: which is Christ in you, the hope of glory."*

Now I am not saying this is a license to sin. Sin is stupid. It opens the door to allow the enemy to attack you with all sorts of evil, and sin has consequences in the natural. However, because God the Father sees you through Jesus, He does not see your sin or bad behavior; He sees Jesus' righteousness. He took your sin and gave you His holiness.

So you can run boldly to your Heavenly Father today and tell Him your needs, desires, and cares. He holds nothing against you. He can't tell you and Jesus apart!

A Prayer for Today

Heavenly Father, this news is too wonderful for me to comprehend. You never cease to amaze me with Your grace. Thank You for Your comprehensive plan that redeemed me so completely. Thank You that You accept me just as readily as You accept Jesus!

Day 67

PROUD DADDY'S CHILD

And suddenly a voice came from heaven, saying, "This is My beloved Son, in whom I am well pleased."

—Matthew 3:17

Four words every child desperately wants to hear from their father is, "I'm proud of you." These are priceless words that can change a life. Sadly, many children grow up without ever hearing those life-affirming, identity-defining words.

Your experience with an earthly father will likely determine how readily you can accept the love of your Heavenly Father. Whether you've had a healthy earthly father relationship or not, your Heavenly Father wants you to know He is your perfect Father. He wants you to experience how deep His love is for you. Even the love of the best human father pales in comparison with your Heavenly Father's love.

Psalm 27:10 (TPT) says, *"My father and mother abandoned me. I'm like an orphan! But you took me in and made me yours."*

Knowing your Heavenly Father's love makes all the difference in the world. Jesus loved Judas (who betrayed Him) as much as He loved John; the difference was that John knew it. In the Gospel of John, the apostle John calls God "Father" 110 times, compared with thirty-eight times for Matthew, five times for Mark, and eleven times for Luke.

Why do you think that is? John always referred to himself as "the disciple whom Jesus loved." He knew he was loved. He could see God as his loving Father.

It is vital to your spiritual growth that you have a profound revelation of your Father God's love for you. Love produces trust. To trust God, you must know beyond a shadow of a doubt that He loves you and is pleased with you.

It is important to note that when Father God announced to the world with a voice from heaven, *"I'm proud of my son,"* it was before Jesus had done any work for God; he was just beginning his ministry. He loved him and was proud of him for who he was, not what he did.

Dear child of God, here's something to celebrate: your Heavenly Father says the same thing about you as He said about His firstborn Son. He loves you and is well pleased with you, too, simply because you believed in His Son, Jesus Christ.

A Prayer for Today

Dear Heavenly Father, open the eyes of my understanding that I may know Your unconditional love and acceptance for me. Heal my heart from any wounds I received from human examples of a father's love or lack of love. I know my earthly father did the best he knew to do. But now I want the revelation of the love of my Heavenly Father. Holy Spirit, teach me to see You as my perfect, loving Father so that I trust You entirely forever.

Day 68

Endlessly Loved Child of God

I have revealed to them who you are and I will continue
to make you even more real to them, so that they may
experience the same endless love that you have for me, for
your love will now live in them, even as I live in them!

—John 17:26 (TPT)

John 17:20–26 is the last recorded prayer that Jesus prayed for you, dear child of God, before He went back to heaven. This prayer reveals the intensity of God's love for you and the grand plan that was put in place for you to be included in Christ Jesus from the very foundation of the world!

Jesus prayed this prayer with you on His mind. Read this prayer and insert your name into the prayer to get a glimpse into Jesus' heart for you and how much you are loved.

Jesus prayed,

And I ask not only for these disciples, but also for _____ and all those who will one day believe in Me through their message. I pray for _____ and all the believers to be joined together as one even as You and I, Father, are joined together as one.

I pray for them to become one with Us so that the world will recognize that You sent me. For the very glory You have given to Me,

I have given _____ and all the believers (my church) so that they will be joined together as one and experience the same unity that We enjoy.

You live fully in me, and now, I live fully in _____ and all the believers so that they will experience perfect unity. And the world will be convinced that You have sent Me, for they will see that You love each one of them with the same passionate love that You have for Me.

Father, I ask that You allow _____, along with all the believers that You have given to Me to be with Me where I am! Then, _____ will see My full glory—the very splendor You have placed upon Me because You have loved Me even before the beginning of time.

You are my righteous Father, but the unbelieving world has never known You in the perfect way that I know You! And _____ and all those who believe in me also know that You have sent Me!

I have revealed to _____ who You are and I will continue to make You even more real to him/her so that _____ may experience the same endless love that You have for Me, for Your love will now live in _____, even as I live in him/her!

A Prayer for Today

Dear Heavenly Father, what amazing truth! Even before You created the world, I was on Your mind. You also knew my name. This truth is too marvelous for me to comprehend, but I sure want to try. Thank You for revealing the reality of Your love for me.

Day 69

CHILDLIKE CHILD OF GOD

*This is why I tell you to never be worried about your life, for all
that you need will be provided, such as food, water, clothing—
everything your body needs. Isn't there more to your life than a meal?
Isn't your body more than clothing? Look at all the birds—do you
think they worry about their existence? They don't plant or reap or
store up food, yet your heavenly Father provides them each with
food. Aren't you much more valuable to your Father than they?*

—Matthew 6:25–26 (TPT)

Children have it easy. They don't worry about buying groceries.
They don't stress over money to pay the electric bill or house
payment. They don't concern themselves with the cost of designer
jeans or new gym shoes. They don't beg their parents to put dinner
on the table or to give them milk money for school. For the most
part, children in America rest in the fact that their parents will take
care of them. Your Heavenly Father wants you to depend on Him
the same way.

This doesn't mean that you sit back and don't work but that you
trust your Father for a job. You trust your Father for grace to handle
your responsibilities. You trust your Father for wisdom and favor for
promotions. You trust your Father for provision. You trust Him to
keep His promises to you.

Matthew 6 goes on to say in verse 31, *"So then, forsake your worries! Why would you say, 'What will we eat?' or 'What will we drink?' or 'What will we wear?' For that is what the unbelievers chase after. Doesn't your heavenly Father already know the things your body requires?"*

You might be thinking, *But, Wendy, God helps those who help themselves.* Do you know that is not a verse in the Bible? Instead, it says, *"But seek first the kingdom of God and His righteousness, and all these things shall be added to you" (Matthew 6:33).*

In other words, seek to know how God's kingdom works. It works by faith. Understand that it's Jesus' blood that made you righteous and acceptable to the Father. Trust your Daddy and come to Him for all you need today.

A Prayer for Today

Dear Daddy, I trust You! Thank You that I don't have to worry because You care for me. You've got me in Your mighty arms today, and You'll never let me go. I love You.

Day 70

STUCK-TOGETHER-LIKE-GLUE CHILD OF GOD

*Christ is the visible image of the invisible God. He
existed before anything was created and is supreme over
all creation… And he holds all creation together.*

—Colossians 1:15, 17

Have you ever heard kids arguing about whose dad is better, stronger, smarter than another? Well, as a child of God, you'll win that debate every time. Your Heavenly Father is greater than any other, and I can prove it.

How inconceivably big and powerful is your Father? He spoke the universe into existence. With a breath from God, He flung huge raging balls of fire, called "stars" into space.

He breathed into man, and he became a living being. He knit human beings together with fascinating detail and wonder; it tells us in Psalm 139.

A look inside the human body reveals the secret glue our Father uses to hold us together. It's called laminins.

Wikipedia describes *laminins* as a *"family of proteins that are an integral part of the structural scaffolding of basement membranes in human tissue."* Literally, they are cell adhesion molecules; they hold one cell to the next cell. But what is mind-blowing is that these laminin structures form the exact shape of the cross!

How profound is that? The glue God created to hold us together is in the shape of the cross. Coincidence? I don't think so!

It is a secret message hidden in every cell of our body that points us to the only way to the Father, through Jesus' cross.

Oh, how your Father loves you. He wants you to know Him. His attention to the most minute detail in your body points you to Him.

Dear child of God, you can be assured that if your Father created you with such attention to detail, that there is nothing that concerns you today that your Daddy cannot or will not handle. Trust Him with all your big and small problems today.

He loves you. The cross makes it obvious.

A Prayer for Today

Dear Creator Daddy, I know that my Father is bigger and better and stronger and smarter and more loving and kind and forgiving than any other father on earth! I win! Thank You, Father, for making me so wonderfully complex. I trust You with every concern in my heart today.

Day 71

STEADFAST-ON-STATUTES CHILD OF GOD

Thus says the Lord, Who gives the sun for a light by day, the ordinances of the moon and the stars for a light by night, Who disturbs the sea, and its waves roar (The Lord of hosts is His name): "If those ordinances depart from before Me, says the Lord, Then the seed of Israel shall also cease from being a nation before Me forever."

—Jeremiah 31:35–36

Did the sun come up this morning? Did you notice the moon last night?

God created five universal ordinances—sun, moon, stars, earth and seas—that are seen around the world to assure us that His Word will never fail. God says just look around you and see His guarantee that the Word of God is settled and does not change.

In Psalm 89:34, God declares, *"My covenant I will not break, nor alter the word that has gone out of My lips."*

Let me remind you again; the formula to receive all God's promises is found in Romans 10:10, *"For with the heart one believes unto righteousness, and with the mouth, confession is made unto salvation."* Believe and confess.

In the appendix to this book, you will find my list of "70 Promises for an Abundant Life." Find the promise that fits your situation today, personalize it, put your name into the promise, and trust God to fulfill it in your life.

Believe in your heart that God's Word is true and is for you. Confess with your mouth the promise you need for today, look down at the earth you are standing on and at the sun above, and expect to receive what God promised you, His child.

Then declare this, "As sure as the sun came up this morning, my answer is on its way!"

A PRAYER FOR TODAY

Dear Father, thank You that You put Your ordinances in the sky and earth that gives me confidence that Your Word remains and will never fail. You've thought of everything!

Day 72

CHILD OF GOD WITH RESERVED SEATING

So David said to him [Mephibosheth], "Do not fear, for I
will surely show you kindness for Jonathan your father's sake,
and will restore to you all the land of Saul your grandfather;
and you shall eat bread at my table continually."

—2 Samuel 9:7

The Bible tells us that Jesus' sacrifice on our behalf fulfilled the Old Testament laws, but still the stories recorded from Genesis to Malachi are beautiful messages of our salvation. In essence, they are living prophecies demonstrating our inheritance in the New Covenant, the favor we have with our King (1 Corinthians 10:11).

One of my favorite historical events in the Old Testament is the story of David and Mephibosheth. After David became king, and the dust had settled, he inquires who is left of his beloved friend Jonathan's family to whom he could show kindness. He learns that Jonathan's son is still alive. In an instance, David offers favor to Mephibosheth and takes him from the pit to the palace. David restores all that he had lost, treats him as part of his family, and insists that from now on, Mephibosheth has a reserved seat at the king's table to eat with the rest of David's sons.

In this story, David is a type of Father God. Jonathan is a type of Jesus, and Jonathan's son Mephibosheth represents you and me.

Mephibosheth had done nothing to earn favor from the king. Still, because of the covenant his father had with David, now David was bestowing Jonathan's inheritance onto his son.

In 2 Samuel 9, David finds Mephibosheth with a severe disability. He is paralyzed in his legs and is living in a town called Lodebar. *Lodebar* means *"place of utter destruction, a place of lack."* That describes our life before Jesus—weak, disabled, hopeless.

David restored Mephibosheth in three areas:

1. His position—King David treats him as one of his sons.
2. His possessions—David returns all the inheritance of land and vineyards to Mephibosheth that his father owned. land the enemy had stolen.
3. His power and authority—David gives him thirty-six servants to farm his land.

Just as David restored Mephibosheth's position, possessions, and power, Jesus has restored you in the same way!

Your Father says to you, "Pull up a chair and eat bread from My table."

As long as Mephibosheth had his chair pulled up to the king's table, he was unaware of his disability. Similarly, as long as you sit up close to Daddy's table, your weaknesses don't show either. Your Father's love and grace provides everything you need for entire restoration.

A PRAYER FOR TODAY

Dear Heavenly Father, thank You for Your tremendous love that has completely restored me to a relationship with You. I declare my days in Lodebar have ended. I have gone from the pit to the palace. I have pulled up my chair to Your table and will never again be without Your favor and power!

Day 73

WISE AND FAVORED CHILD OF GOD

Let not mercy and truth forsake thee: bind them about thy neck;
write them upon the table of thine heart: So shalt thou find
favor and good understanding in the sight of God and man.

—Proverbs 3:3–4 (KJV)

"*I have favor with God, favor with man and a good understanding.*"
This is a powerful declaration to make about yourself every day!

One of my instructors at Charis Bible College told a story about a child that was failing in school. The father told him to start declaring every day *"I have favor with God, favor with man, and a good understanding."* Before long, instead of getting the lowest grade in the class, his grades were among the highest. He started believing what he was saying, and it changed his results!

As Jesus grew from childhood to an adult, it says in Luke 2:52 that *"Jesus increased in wisdom and stature, and in favor with God and man."*

How did Jesus increase in wisdom as a child? By his daily reading of the Holy Scriptures.

He discovered His identity and the truth about His destiny by reading Isaiah and the prophets. I'm sure His mother, Mary, would have tucked Him in bed at night telling Him the story of how the angel came to her and told her she would have a son, name Him

Jesus, and that He would be the Savior of the world. I can imagine that Jesus never tired of hearing the story over and over again of the angels announcing His birth to the shepherds. Mary would have explained to Him that God was His true Father, not Joseph. He grew in this wisdom and truth by studying the scriptures that confirmed her stories.

This is how you grow in wisdom and favor too. The enemy is working overtime to try to get you to doubt your acceptance by God. He'll whisper lies attempting to make you question the truth about who God says you are and whether God can be trusted.

That's why it is so important to know the truth and "bind it around your neck." It is critical in today's world that you understand what your Father says about you, that you know your identity, your inheritance and your influence.

So today, plant the Word of God in your heart. Keep it close to you and declare that you have favor with God, favor with man, and a good understanding!

A Prayer for Today

Heavenly Father, in a world with lies and deception all around me, thank You that Your Word tells me the truth about who I am. I am Your favored child with good understanding. I am determined to keep Your Word in front of me always. I choose to guard my heart and filter everything I hear today by the truth of Your Word.

Day 74

Tongue-Powered Child of God

Death and life are in the power of the tongue,
and those who love it will eat its fruit.

—Proverbs 18:21

Yesterday I suggested that you declare "I have favor with God, favor with man, and a good understanding."

According to our verse for today, there is great power in what you say; in fact, what you say is a matter of life or death!

I hate to admit it, but my husband and I are hooked on this TV series called *Heartland*. We're on the 219th episode! On a recent show, Mallory was taking riding lessons. At most, she weighed fifty pounds. The horse probably weighed about 1,200 pounds. However, this little gal directed the horse wherever she wanted it to go with just a bridle in the horse's mouth.

Just as she turned the horse with simple pressure on its mouth, you can turn your life around with the words of your mouth. I challenge you to take an assessment:

- What are you saying about yourself?
- What are you saying about your financial situation?
- What are you saying about your spouse?
- What are you saying about your kids?

- What are you saying about your job?

If you don't like the results you see in your life, change what you are saying about it.

When someone asks, "How are you," rather than responding with an assessment of how you feel in the natural—for instance, "I'm okay," "I'm hanging in there," "Not great," "My allergies are acting up today," "I'm having a bad day"—instead, say what God says about you according to His Word: "I am on top and not the bottom. I am greatly blessed, highly favored, and deeply loved. I am having a very productive day because everything I put my hands to do prospers! The Healer lives in me, so I am healed in Jesus' name."

You might be thinking that saying positive things about your life when you only see negative seems like lying, but God is your example. Romans 4:17 says, *"God, who gives life to the dead and calls those things which do not exist as though they did."*

Choose to believe God's promises and speak yourself into a great day today!

A Prayer for Today

Heavenly Father, I'm Your child, so of course, I speak and create like my Father—with my words. Teach me to realize the power in my words. Holy Spirit, remind me to guard my tongue and speak life—always.

Day 75

BENEFIT-ENDOWED CHILD OF GOD

Bless the Lord, O my soul, and forget not all His benefits: Who forgives all your iniquities and Who heals all your diseases, Who redeems your life from destruction, Who crowns you with lovingkindness and tender mercies, Who satisfies your mouth with good things so that your youth is renewed like the eagles.

—Psalm 103:2–3

Let's imagine it's Christmas morning. You have beautifully wrapped gifts piled high under the tree. You can hardly wait to see the delight on your kids' faces when they realize every item on their wish list is theirs. So how would you feel if they ignored your gifts and left them wrapped and untouched? It would be heartbreaking, right?

Likewise, it grieves your Heavenly Father when you leave gifts under Calvary's tree, gifts especially bought for you that Jesus purchased with His own holy, sinless blood.

One of the gifts Jesus purchased for you at the cross that is often left unopened is healing. Note in today's verse, forgiveness of sin and healing of diseases are both in the same sentence! If you can believe your sins are forgiven, you can believe for healing. Jesus purchased both for you as a package deal.

God wants you well. It's His character. Everywhere Jesus went in His earthly ministry, He healed all who came to Him. There wasn't a single incident where He said no. Most people believe God is able to heal but wonder if He is willing.

There was a leper who came to Jesus with the same thought. In Matthew 8:2, it says, *"And behold, a leper came and worshiped Him, saying, 'Lord, if You are willing, You can make me clean.'"* I love Jesus' answer. *"Then Jesus put out His hand and touched him, saying, 'I am willing; be cleansed.' Immediately his leprosy was cleansed."* The Hebrew word translated *willing* in this verse actually means "continually and always willing"!

Jesus never changes. He was willing to heal then, and He is willing to heal you today. In fact, it was already finished at the cross!

So if you are struggling with sickness today, from coronavirus to cancer, God's healing power is available for you. It's a gift He's waiting for you to unwrap. Accept the gift. Believe it is yours. You receive healing in the same way you received forgiveness for your sins, believing it's yours and confessing it by faith (Romans 10:9–10).

Healing is a gift under the tree with your name on it!

A Prayer for Today

Dear Heavenly Father, everything I need for today I find in You. Thank You for all the benefits that are mine just because I am Your child. I take the gift of Your healing into my body today. You have truly blessed me and empowered me to prosper in every way.

Day 76

Loved-Beyond-Measure Child of God

Endless love beyond measurement that transcends our understanding—this extravagant love pours into you until you are filled to overflowing with the fullness of God!

—Ephesians 3:19 (TPT)

Knowing the unconditional love of our Heavenly Father is the bedrock of the Christian faith. Here are some marvelous truths that demonstrate how much God loves you personally.

God loved you when you were at your ugliest.

> *But God showed his great love for us by sending Christ to die for us while we were still sinners. (Romans 5:8)*

My husband, Don, and I were dating when I was diagnosed with a brain tumor which required immediate surgery. Following the operation, my head swelled up like a balloon, my eyes looked dark and sullen, and Don described my appearance similar to the "elephant man." But it was at this point when I was looking my absolute

175

ugliest that God told him to marry me! I think the timing was perfect because no matter how old, gray, cellulite-infested, and wrinkled I might become with age, I'll never look as ugly as the day he decided to marry me!

It was at our ugliest that God saw our value, loved us, and chose to rescue and redeem us too!

Here are some more truths about God's love for you:

You are so valuable to God that He was willing to give up everything He had to redeem you.

> *For you know that God paid a ransom to save you from the empty life you inherited from your ancestors. And it was not paid with mere gold or silver, which lose their value. It was the precious blood of Christ, the sinless, spotless Lamb of God. (1 Peter 1:18–19)*

His love gave you His best, so all the rest is yours too.

> *What shall we say about such wonderful things as these? If God is for us, who can ever be against us? Since he did not spare even his own Son but gave him up for us all, won't he also give us everything else? (Romans 8:31–32, NLT)*

Meditating on these truths will fill up your love meter. Intimately knowing God's love for you will remove all fear and doubt and allow you to stand confidently in faith to receive everything you need from your loving Father's hand. As it says in 1 John 4:18, that "*perfect love drives out fear.*"

A Prayer for Today

> *Father God, Your love for me is too marvelous to comprehend! I trust in Your love for me. I know that I have no reason to fear or doubt Your promises because You love me.*

Day 77

HOLY AND ACCEPTED CHILD OF GOD

For it was always in his perfect plan to adopt us as his delightful children, through our union with Jesus, the Anointed One, so that his tremendous love that cascades over us would glorify his grace—for the same love he has for his Beloved One, Jesus, he has for us. And this unfolding plan brings him great pleasure!

—Ephesians 1:5–6 (TPT)

God loves you with the same love He has for Jesus. God is flat out excited about you!

He's not mad at you; He is not holding your sins against you. *"That God was in Christ reconciling the world to Himself, not imputing their trespasses to them"* (2 Corinthians 5:19a).

Nothing you do will ever make Him love you less. On the other hand, nothing you do can make Him love you more.

My husband and I shared these truths with one of our grandsons recently. He felt like he didn't deserve God's love and acceptance because of some bad choices he had made in his life.

We knew he had accepted Jesus Christ as his Savior and Lord, so we reminded him that Jesus took all his sins past, present, and future. The good news is that God is not counting his sins against him anymore!

God is not counting your sins against you either, dear child of God.

Sin allows the enemy to get a hold in your life, so it's just smart to stay away from sin. But as far as God's concerned, when He looks at you, He sees Jesus' blood sacrifice, not your sin. He determines you to be holy and acceptable to Him. That's amazing grace!

The word *accepted* in Ephesians 1:6 (KJV) is the same word that is translated in Luke 1:28, "highly favored," when the angel announces to Mary that she is blessed among women and was chosen to be the virgin mother of the Savior of the world.

Do you feel undeserving of God's love today? Have you made a mess in your life, and now you feel unworthy to pray and ask for God's help to fix the situation?

Remember that it is Jesus who made you holy and accepted—there's nothing you do to deserve it except believe! He is saying to you today that you are His "highly favored" one.

So relax. Rest in God's grace. Your Father is waiting for you to ask for His help.

A Prayer for Today

Heavenly Father, thank You for Your amazing grace! Regardless of how my flesh feels today, I accept the truth that You approve of me because of Jesus. In Jesus' name, I receive all the promises that You say belong to me today because salvation includes forgiveness, healing, restoration, safety, provision, and wholeness.

Day 78

LIFE-CHOOSING CHILD OF GOD

*Today, I have given you the choice between life and death,
between blessings and curses. Now I call on heaven and
earth to witness the choice you make. Oh, that you would
choose life, so that you and your descendants might live!*

—Deuteronomy 30:19 (NLT)

During the three years that I attended Charis Bible College, I took many exams. Whether we realize it or not, we take tests every single day.

I guarantee that before this day is over, you'll face the multiple-choice test of Deuteronomy 30:19. Do you choose blessings? cursings? life? or death?

Your Father, who loves you, has already slipped you the correct answer. He says, *"Choose life so that you and your family might live."*

The dilemma comes when you face a problem or temptation in your life and decide to handle it independently. You make your decision based on desire, fear, or human logic.

Acting on your own is what the devil hopes you'll do. It's a sure win for him. It leaves you powerless without your Father's help.

For example, let's say you have a cousin coming to visit, and you have been tempted to take offense at them for making a critical remark about you at the last family reunion—you need grace to be able to treat them with love and let go of the offense. You could claim Hebrews 4:16, *"Let us therefore come boldly to the throne of grace, that we may obtain mercy and find grace to help in time of need."* Standing on this promise you could pray, "Lord, I can't love my cousin on my own. I am coming to your throne for some grace. I receive your grace for every situation and conversation with my cousin today."

You choose life and blessings by believing God's Word, believing what God has promised you and believing in the authority God has given you as His child and ambassador on earth.

A Prayer for Today

I choose to believe that I can do all things through Christ, which strengthens me. I choose to believe that my Father rescues the children of the godly. I choose to believe that Jesus took all my sickness on the cross, and by His stripes, I was healed. I choose to believe that my God supplies all my needs. I choose life!

Day 79

CHILD OF GOD WHO MAKES DADDY DANCE

For the LORD your God is living among you. He is a mighty savior.
He will take delight in you with gladness. With His love, He will
calm all your fears. He will rejoice over you with joyful songs.

—Zephaniah 3:17 (NLT)

God is making a big commotion over you in heaven. Just the mere thought of you inspires God Himself to twirl around and sing and rejoice!

I love my children, but I've ever been so enthusiastic or demonstrative about my love for them to cause me to let go and dance a jig.

But that is how delighted God is about you.

In Zephaniah 3:17, *"rejoice over you"* in the Hebrew means to "spin around in joy under violent emotion" or basically to dance. God dances with shouts of joy over you!

I love this verse. The prophet describes the deep and abiding love God has for you. God is with you. He is your mighty Savior who forgives, heals, restores, provides, protects. God cares for you. You are a treasure to Him. God pays attention to every detail of your life.

God's Word Translation says it this way: *"The LORD, your God, is with you. He is a hero who saves you. He happily rejoices over you, renews you with his love, and celebrates over you with shouts of joy."*

The Amplified Version reads: *"The Lord your God is in your midst, a Warrior who saves. He will rejoice over you with joy; He will be quiet in His love [making no mention of your past sins], He will rejoice over you with shouts of joy."*

Take a moment to bask in your Father's love for you today. Give all your cares to Him, then dance and rejoice with the One who loves you, holds no sin against you, and meets all your needs.

A Prayer for Today

Dear Father, You are my hero! I am so humbled to realize that You are singing and dancing at the very thought of me today. Wow! What love. I love You because You first loved me.

Day 80

Empowered for Healing
Child of God

Now it happened on a certain day, as He was teaching, that there were Pharisees and teachers of the law sitting by, who had come out of every town of Galilee, Judea, and Jerusalem. And the power of the Lord was present to heal them.

—Luke 5:17

Healing is a contentious topic in churches today. Some people believe that God can heal but don't believe it's always His will to heal. Some think healing miracles ended with the apostles. But the happy (and healed) folks like me are those who believe that God is always willing to heal and that healing is as much our right today as it ever has been. It is part of our salvation package. In Psalm 103:2-3, the psalmist reminds us to, *"Bless the Lord, O my soul, And forget not all His benefits: Who forgives all your iniquities, Who heals all your diseases."* But as the saying goes, "Believe and receive, or doubt and do without."

A lot of the debate on healing stems from the misinterpretation of scripture. For example, in today's verse, "And the power of the Lord was *present* to heal them," implies that the power to heal can come and go. On this particular day when Jesus was teaching, healing power seemed to be *present*. But the word *present* is not in the original text; that is why it is italicized in this translation, showing the author added it. But the word "present" has no business being present in this verse!

Young's Literal Translation accurately reads: *"and the power of the Lord was to heal them."*

The power of the Lord is to heal.

Here's the good news: as a child of God, God's power lives in you, so healing power is available to you 24/7. He has promised never to leave you or forsake you!

The word translated as "power" is dunamis in the original Greek, which is the inherent, strength, ability, miracle-working power of God. It's where we get the word dynamite or dynamo.

Do you need healing today? The dynamite power of the Lord is in you, to heal you. You've got it. Receive it the same way you received forgiveness for your sins—by faith.

A Prayer for Today

Father God, by faith, I declare, I am empowered with Your healing power, so my body is a perfect health zone! I will continue in faith, believing to see manifest in my body what's already done in my spirit. No sickness, virus, or malfunction is allowed in my body. I am whole and healed and live in health and prosperity!

Day 81

COMMUNING CHILD OF GOD

For as often as you eat this bread and drink this cup, you
proclaim the Lord's death till He comes. Therefore, whoever
eats this bread or drinks this cup of the Lord in an unworthy
manner will be guilty of the body and blood of the Lord.

—1 Corinthians 11:26–27

When I was a teenager, I was just a tad bit rebellious. If my mother heard me tell you this, she would scoff and say, "You're the reason my hair turned gray at such a young age!"

But praise God, I've been redeemed and transformed!

However, in my teen years, I was definitely a backslidden Christian. I think my mother had my name on every prayer chain in town!

At the Baptist church we attended, communion was served the first Sunday of every month. Before the ushers passed the bread and grape juice, the pastor would read the warning found in the last sentence of today's scripture.

This word scared me. Often I would make up an excuse of an urgent need to run to the restroom. I knew I was in the "unworthy" category and was sure that if I partook I would get sick or struck by lightning.

But fortunately, since then, I've learned the true meaning of this warning. Communion is a beautiful gift that Jesus demonstrated to the disciples before leaving for heaven. As often as we eat this meal, it is a reminder to us of the inheritance that Jesus bought for us at the cross!

Sadly, in the majority of churches, communion is just a ritual. In 1 Corinthians 11:29–30, Paul tells us clearly that one reason some Christians are weak and sick and die prematurely is that they don't discern the Lord's body when they partake of the holy Communion.

You partake in an unworthy manner—when you make communion a ritual without honoring Christ's body and realizing its power to heal and make you whole.

When Jesus held up the bread at the Lord's Supper, Jesus said, *"This is my body, broken for you."* The bread represents that Jesus' body was broken and beaten for our health and healing.

> *Surely He has borne our griefs and carried our sorrows; yet we esteemed Him stricken, smitten by God, and afflicted. But He was wounded for our transgressions, He was bruised for our iniquities; the chastisement for our peace was upon Him, and by His stripes, we are healed.* (Isaiah 53:4–5)

To discern Jesus' body is to apply the truth of what Jesus accomplished through the horrendous pain and suffering He endured at the cross and the sacrifice He paid to redeem you. Eating the bread is literally ingesting the power of God to heal you, the power to bless you, the power to restore you and bring you wholeness.

Every child of God who has received Jesus' gift of salvation is worthy to take communion. Jesus made you righteous and worthy. Once again, Jesus did all the work; your part is to believe and receive all He has done for you!

A PRAYER FOR TODAY

Heavenly Father, thank You for this special covenant meal that reminds me of Your grace and goodness and Your complete finished work for me at Calvary. I trust in your forgiveness for those times I've taken this meal lightly, without realizing the true meaning of your body, broken for me. I receive Your healing power and sacrifice of Your body, into my body for complete healing and wholeness today.

Day 82

BLOOD-COVENANT-SEALED CHILD OF GOD

In the same manner He also took the cup after supper, saying, "This cup is the new covenant in My blood. This do, as often as you drink it, in remembrance of Me." For as often as you eat this bread and drink this cup, you proclaim the Lord's death till He comes.

—1 Corinthians 11:25–26

Jesus invites us to come to His table whenever we wish. It's not a ritual; it is a fellowship time with Jesus, a time to express your co-union with Him, identify yourself with your Savior and claim your inheritance in the finished work of Jesus Christ.

Most Christians are aware that the cup of wine represents Jesus' blood that paid the penalty for our sins. But living the abundant life God promises you starts with recognizing that Jesus' blood enforces the new covenant that Father God cut with Jesus on your behalf. It is this knowledge that gives you confidence to receive all God's promises and the inheritance that belongs to you as a co-heir with Jesus, right here on earth. It is this covenant that gives you more than a ticket to heaven!

Then, looking ahead to meeting your Father in heaven, the blood represented through the cup, also ensures that Jesus has the exceeding great joy of presenting you faultless and blameless before the throne of God!

So take communion often. You don't have to be in church to do it. Your priest or pastor isn't the only one who is authorized to serve it.

Jesus put no stipulations on how this meal was to be served. He simply instructed His children eat often and let it remind you of Jesus' finished work at the cross and the covenant He bought us.

My husband and I take communion often right at our kitchen table. Whenever the devil tries to put sickness on us or when we have a financial need or are asking God's direction in a specific issue, we remind ourselves of the covenant we have with our Heavenly Father and enforce its power. We remember through the bread and wine that we have a covenant for all the gifts of salvation, not just forgiveness but also healing, prosperity, deliverance, safety, rescue, liberation, restoration.

I took communion with my friend who had been struggling with an irregular heartbeat. She told me later that after we enforced the covenant and the healing that belonged to her, she knew she was healed. She began to improve from that day forward, and today, she has a healthy heart.

Here's a sample prayer for communion:

Get out a cracker and wine or grape juice—we've even used water and a cookie. (Remember, Jesus turned water into wine! What the elements represent is what matters.)

Look at the bread in your hand. Imagine Jesus on the cross. Picture yourself taking your knee pain, or cancer, or disease symptoms and putting it on Jesus' body. He took it all on Himself. He carried your sickness to the grave but rose without it! So pray:

> Thank You, Jesus, for Your broken body. Thank You for taking all my symptoms and sickness, poverty and lack into Your body at the cross so that I can have Your health and wholeness. I declare that by Your stripes, by the beatings You bore, by the whip that fell on Your back, I am completely healed. I believe and I

receive Your resurrection life in my body today. (Eat the bread.)

Then take the cup in your hand and pray,

Thank You, Jesus, for Your precious blood that You willingly poured out to cleanse me of all my sin, past, present, and future. Thank you for making me righteous, accepted by God. This cup represents Your blood which seals the covenant that You and Father God cut on my behalf. As I drink, I celebrate and partake of the inheritance You guarantee for me through the covenant in Your blood. This includes provision, restoration, and wholeness in every area of my life. (Drink the cup.)

A Prayer for Today

Lord Jesus, You knew I'd need a reminder! Thank You for this extraordinary meal that reminds me of Your extraordinary love and sacrifice and all You've bought me. I never want to let one drop of Your precious blood go to waste. I love You.

Day 83

BLESSED HEIR OF GOD

By his divine power, God has given us everything we need for living a godly life. We have received all of this by coming to know him, the one who called us to himself by means of his marvelous glory and excellence.

—2 Peter 1:3 (NLT)

There are two kinds of Christians in our world today: those who are blessed and believe it and those who are blessed and don't believe it.

What would you do if you received a registered letter announcing that your wealthy aunt had died and had named you as her sole heir in her will? How long would it take you to run to the court and claim your inheritance? I bet you'd break the speed limit getting there!

It is your responsibility as an heir of Jesus Christ to believe you are blessed and claim your inheritance. If you don't believe it, the devil will be happy to steal it from you.

All the promises throughout the Word of God belong to you. In the appendix of this book, you'll find "70 Promises for an Abundant Life." This is just a sampling of all God promises that belong to you as His child. There are actually over eight thousand promises in God's Word—I am sure you'll find what you are looking for!

It is an insult to your Father to ask Him for what He's already promised is yours. If you have a habit of praying, "God be with me today." Stop that, dear friend. It is insulting to God. He has already promised that He will never leave you or forsake you. Instead, pray, *"Thank You, Father, that You are with me today. You are leading me to make the right decisions. I am never afraid because You are with me."*

Simply start acknowledging the good things that the Word says are yours, and then your faith will become effective.

Your Father already knows what you need and wants you to have it. God has already forgiven you, already healed you. He's already commanded His blessing upon you and your finances, already given you love, joy, and peace.

So bottom line: it is not a matter of trying to get God to move in your life; it's a matter of you moving into agreement with Him and receiving what He has already provided.

A Prayer for Today

Dear Amazing Father, thank You for Your patience with me while I grow in understanding of what was purchased for me and belongs to me because of Jesus! I'm sorry for begging when I should have simply been receiving what You've already provided for me. From now on, I am taking You at your Word and claiming the inheritance that is mine. Wow! How You've lavished Your love on me!

Day 84

FIRED-UP CHILD OF GOD

Therefore I remind you to stir up the gift of God which is in you through the laying on of my hands. For God has not given us a spirit of fear, but of power and of love and of a sound mind.

—2 Timothy 1:6–7

Did you wake up this morning feeling like God was a long way off? Do you feel tired and alone? Do you feel fear or dread about a situation? Are you feeling discouraged?

I've been there.

In those times, I've found it is crucial to take the advice Apostle Paul gave to Timothy, *"Stir up the gift of God, which is in you."*

"You stir yourself up," Paul says. It is your responsibility. "Stir up" is a phrase that evokes stirring up embers in a fire so they will not go out. The Amplified Bible says it this way, *"Rekindle the embers of, fan the flame of, and keep burning."* God gives us the flame, but we control how hot it gets.

To get the fire burning hot, you must daily remind yourself of your identity and your inheritance.

Child of God, here is some "kindling" to stir up your fire today. Meditate on these truths about you:

You have been made righteous.

You are a temple of God.
You have the mind of Christ.
You are anointed by God.
You have favor with God, favor with man, and a good understanding.
God planned for you even before the creation of the world.
You lack no good thing.
You have an abundance for every good work.
God predestined you for success.
Your family is blessed, your flocks are blessed, every-thing you touch prospers.
You are the head and not the tail, above the circum-stances, not beneath them.
The blessings of the Lord encircle you, go before you, and overtake you![1]

And those are just a few to get you started!

When you stir yourself up to remember what God says is true about you, then fear and discouragement will leave and you will feel energized, bold, and confident. You will recognize the power in you, God's love for you, and remember the truth of who you are as a child of God.

A Prayer for Today

Dear Father, Your Word is the fire in my bones! Thank You for reminding me that my identity is in Christ. What grace You have bestowed on me that I would be called a child of God. Help me live in the truth of Your Word today.

---

[1]   Second Corinthians 5:21; 1 Corinthians 6:19; 1 Corinthians 2:16; 1 John 2:27; Luke 2:52; Ephesians 1:4; Psalm 34:10; 2 Corinthians 9:8; Romans 8:28–30; Deuteronomy 28:4–8; Deuteronomy 28:13; Deuteronomy 28:2.

Day 85

CONDEMNATION-BUSTING CHILD OF GOD

"No weapon formed against you shall prosper, and every tongue which rises against you in judgment you shall condemn. This is the heritage of the servants of the Lord. And their righteousness is from Me," says the Lord.

—Isaiah 54:17

Hanging from the monkey bars on the playground at North Ward Grade School in Wahoo, Nebraska, I remember my retort to the bully, "Sticks and stones may break my bones, but names will never hurt me."

Kids can be brutal at name-calling. But that little ditty I used to comfort myself is the farthest thing from the truth. Names, words, labels can hurt or ruin your life.

You've probably heard that you should never attach a negative name or label to a child. Never call a child dumb or special needs, autistic or slow learner. Why? It says in Proverbs 18:21, *"Death and life are in the power of the tongue."*

Has someone tried to put a label on you? Loser, hopeless, life-threatening illness, inadequate, failure, poverty-stricken, trouble-maker, black sheep?

It is easy to start believing a name you've been called or treat someone according to a label they've been given. But I have good news for you. You can break the power of those negative words. Whether someone spoke negatively to you, or you naively spoke destructive, death words over yourself or your children, you can fix that.

As a child of God, your inheritance includes the power and authority to condemn every word, every lie that comes against you. *"And every tongue which rises against you in judgment* **you** *shall condemn."*

This verse does not say that God will remove the negative words; it says that you have the power and authority to condemn them. Make the decision to steer clear of the negative and speak life every where you go!

A PRAYER FOR TODAY

I bind every word from my mouth that has released the enemy or drawn weapons against me, in Jesus' name. I bind every hindering force that I've ever given strength to through the ignorance of my own words or that someone has spoken against me. I break the power of those spiritual forces in Jesus' name!

Day 86

OVERCOMING CHILD OF GOD

Who is the one who overcomes the world, but he who believes that
Jesus is the Son of God? For whatever is born of God overcomes the
world; and this is the victory that has overcome the world—our faith.

—1 John 5:4–5

D o you realize that as a child of God, you have devil-defeating,
mountain-moving, world-overcoming power on the inside of
you? God says—you do!

However, if you fail to renew your mind to your true identity
in Christ, it's like going into battle in your underwear. And a naked,
unarmed soldier is not much of a threat to the enemy!

Ephesians 6:11 says, *"Put on the whole armor of God, that you*
may be able to stand against the wiles of the devil."

So get dressed in your armor. Every day declare your inheritance
and identity. Believe and receive it as part of your "salvation benefits
package!"

For the next several days, I'll be sharing how to get yourself
dressed with each piece of God's armor to win the battle every time.

The most crucial piece of armor is the helmet of salvation.
Receiving the gift of salvation that Jesus Christ bought for you at the
cross is the first and most essential step to living victoriously. There is
no power until you plug into the Power Source!

In addition to protecting your head from injury, the helmet also guards your thinking center. Your success in standing against the enemy's lies and schemes is determined by what you think. Are you thinking about who God says you are? Your place in God's family? Your authority as His child? God's promises to you? Whenever you let down your guard and believe lies the enemy wins. Proverbs 23:7 says, "*As a man thinks in his heart, so is he.*" Your thinking will determine if you are a victim or a victor!

God has provided all you need to overcome every trial, every challenge, and crisis that comes across your path. Never allow yourself to be under the circumstances. Guard your thinking and stand victoriously on top all the time!

A Prayer for Today

Dear Father, I firmly strap on the helmet of salvation and ask you, Holy Spirit, to be my lie detector. Help me identify the schemes and lies of the enemy so I am always on top in every situation and only believe Your truth. I am an overcomer!

Day 87

ARMOR-CLAD CHILD OF GOD

*Put on the new self, created after the likeness of
God in true righteousness and holiness.*

—Ephesians 4:24

Yesterday we began focusing on the importance of putting on the whole *armor of God*, starting with the helmet of salvation.

The second piece of armor is the *breastplate of righteousness*.

In ancient Rome, the breastplate was the central part of the Roman soldier's armor—it protected the torso, which contains vital organs like the heart, lungs and kidneys. Without a breastplate, a soldier's chance of victory against his enemy was slim. On the other hand, with a sturdy breastplate, the attacks become ineffective as the arrows ricochet off the armor.

For the child of God, righteousness is your God-given identity. At the launch of Jesus' ministry, while He was in the wilderness fasting for forty days, Satan attacked His identity. He basically said, "If you really are the Son of God…prove it!" Knowing your identity shields you from the attacks from the enemy. The breastplate is critical armor for the dangerous and deceptive times we are living in right now.

You have been *made* righteous and accepted by Jesus Christ (Romans 5:1).

Just as Satan tried to get Jesus to question His identity, he'll try the same thing with you. He'll bring up past sins, remind you of times you've failed, suggest you haven't been reading your Bible enough, prayed enough, or point out that you missed church last week. He'll whisper in your ear that God is mad at you. Taking in his lies begins a downward spiral. You'll start questioning your acceptance by God. Then you won't enforce your victory over the devil, and he'll get away with murder (John 10:10).

Your *breastplate of righteousness* is firmly fastened when you know in your heart without a doubt that you are accepted by God because of Jesus' blood alone and nothing you can do will change that. Jesus made you righteous! This assurance will make you unshakeable and give you the confidence to stand up to the most violent attack, enforcing your inheritance and your victory every time.

A Prayer for Today

Heavenly Father, there is nothing I can do to earn your acceptance except believe in Your Son, Jesus. I rest in the truth that Jesus alone made me righteous and accepted by You. Thank you, Jesus, for exchanging my sin and imperfections for your holiness before Father God! My acceptance and victory are totally because of You!

Day 88

BUCKLED-UP CHILD OF GOD

Stand your ground, putting on the belt of truth
and the body armor of God's righteousness.

—Ephesians 6:14 (NLT)

Today, we put on the belt of truth. I think of it like the thick leather belt a mover uses when lifting heavy furniture. The strap keeps his back strong and supported so he doesn't fall under the weight and hurt himself. You buckle the belt of truth by applying the truth of God's Word. When you make it a habit to read and meditate daily on the Word of God, you are putting on the belt of truth, which strengthens your spiritual backbone and keeps you steady under pressure.

Jesus demonstrated the power of knowing and applying the truth of God's Word at the beginning of His ministry. After forty days of fasting, Jesus was hungry. Matthew 4:3–4 reads, *"Now when the tempter came to Him, he said, 'If You are the Son of God, command that these stones become bread.' But He answered and said, 'It is written, "Man shall not live by bread alone, but by every Word that proceeds from the mouth of God."'"*

A dear Christian friend called me recently asking for prayer. She was fighting back the tears as she told me she and her husband had just left the doctor's office where they had received the news that her husband had prostate cancer. I could tell she was angry and gripped in fear. She said, "I've been begging God to heal him. Maybe it's just not God's will."

I stopped her midsentence. I can't stand to hear people repeat the enemy's lies out loud. I had to help her buckle up her belt of truth! I asked her to show me one time when Jesus ever let anyone stay sick who came to him for healing. When did he ever say, "No, this sickness is good for you?"

Yes, the doctor's report showed cancer. We don't deny the facts, but we reject the ability for the facts to trump the truth. Facts change; God's truth never changes!

I reminded her that she doesn't have to beg God for what already belongs to her as a child of God. The truth says it is always God's will to heal (Matthew 8:2–3). God promises that we will live out the length of our days in health and prosperity (Proverbs 4:10). Healing is part of salvation (Psalm 130:3). And by the stripes of Jesus, her husband was healed at the cross (Isaiah 53:5).

Whether you've got a battle brewing in your health, finances, a relationship, or you're struggling to stay in peace in this fearful world, find my list of God's promises in the appendix of this book. Take hold of the promise you need and cinch up your belt of truth by driving the truth of God's Word deep into your spirit. When you do, you tie down the loose garments of deception and fear that can get you tangled up during the battle. Jesus has already won the battle on your behalf. Stand in that Truth!

A Prayer for Today

Heavenly Father, I put on the belt of truth. You, Father, are Truth. Your word is Truth. Jesus, my Savior, is the Way, the Truth, and the Life. Holy Spirit, teach me to understand my identity and my inheritance—the truth of who I am in Christ. Your truth is eternal. Facts and doctor's reports change. I know the truth, and it sets me free.

Day 89

PEACE-WITHOUT-COMPROMISE CHILD OF GOD

Stand therefore, having girded your waist with truth, having put on the breastplate of righteousness, and having shod your feet with the preparation of the gospel of peace.

—Ephesians 6:14–15

Put on your *peace shoes.*

The apostle Paul's analogy of dressing for battle is very appropriate for today. We are facing enemies, cancel culture, and persecution that we have never witnessed before in America. The shoes referred to in this verse are battle shoes with spikes in the soles allowing the soldier to stand firm and not be moved from the truth of the Gospel of peace.

At Jesus' birth, when the angels announced "peace on earth, goodwill toward men," this was not a declaration that Jesus was bringing world peace. Quite the contrary. The peace Jesus brought was vertical peace between God and man. In Matthew 10:34, Jesus said, *"Perhaps you think I've come to spread peace and calm over the earth—but my coming will bring conflict and division, not peace."*

The society we live in today promotes a far different method of peace than the peace we enjoy with our Heavenly Father. It's a culture that says "we'll have peace as long as you don't step on my toes." A culture that ridicules voicing a biblical worldview or suggesting an unborn baby has as much right to life as its mother.

The Bible says we are to pursue peace with all men as much as possible. But in these days, we must also be aware that God's Word brings division. It divides the sheep and the goats, darkness and light, Christ-followers from those who are anti-Christ.

Pursuing peace does not mean compromise. We cannot have peace with those who celebrate the shedding of innocent lives, abusing children, canceling free speech, or calling biblical truths "hate speech." We will never have peace with those who promote acts of violence or hate our God and His values. We must speak up.

Peace was a challenge in Paul's day too. Standing up for truth brought persecution, but the apostle Paul said in Romans 1:16, *"For I am not ashamed of the gospel of Christ, for it is the power of God to salvation for everyone who believes."* This is where your influence as a child of God becomes powerful!

Today, more than ever, people are desperate for God's kind of peace and for righteous leaders to stand up to the tyranny of those scheming to destroy American freedom. The Gospel is the good news that Jesus freed us from bondage to sin and made us acceptable to God. That's something to shout about! Lace up your peace shoes and take every opportunity to stand up and speak up to defend our freedoms and share God's peace with others.

A Prayer for Today

Heavenly Father, I ask for boldness and courage to stand for You, pursuing peace but never at the cost of compromise. Everywhere I go, I pray that I will leave footprints of the good news of Jesus. Because of Jesus' obedience to the cross, I enjoy a life of abundance, joy, peace, love, provision, and health. Holy Spirit, help me to share this life-changing news with everyone who will listen.

Day 90

FAITH-SHIELDED CHILD OF GOD

Above all, taking the shield of faith with which you will be able to quench all the fiery arrows of the wicked one.

—Ephesians 6:16

Previously, I wrote that I received a bad report from my ophthalmologist. The test results showed age-related macular degeneration (AMD). When I got the news, I immediately identified this as a ploy of the enemy; this was not something God brought on me to teach me a lesson.

You'll never hear me say "I have AMD." AMD is not mine. It violates the covenant I have with my Heavenly Father as a child of God. So I won't take ownership of it.

Often when people talk about a health issue, you will hear them take ownership by saying "my cancer," "my diabetes," "my arthritis is acting up." It's not yours. It belongs to the enemy. So don't accept it!

What I say is: "I was diagnosed with AMD, but God's Word says by the stripes of Jesus, I was healed—so I am expecting my vision to be totally restored."

It is vital that you hold on tight to your *shield of faith*. Faith is the currency of the kingdom of God and is the only defense you need. Faith is the victory!

Psalm 91:4 tells us, *"His Truth is your shield and buckler."* God's truth provides two types of shields—a big body shield, and the buckler, a smaller moveable shield so you are covered against the enemy's attack from head to toe.

The enemy continually seeks to attack you by shooting arrows of doubt, temptation, worry, and deception into your heart and mind, tempting you to let go of God's promises to you. Fear will cause you to drop your shield, and the enemy will begin to win. Whether you are claiming God's promises for your health, for protection, or a new job, put your shields in place by renewing your mind on the Truth and standing in faith.

A Prayer for Today

Heavenly Father, You are greater in me than the enemy who is in the world. I firmly grasp my shield of faith and do not waiver in unbelief. With the truth of your Word, I quench every attack of the enemy and receive all you promise me.

Day 91

Dressed-for-Success Child of God

For the Word of God is alive and powerful. It is sharper than the sharpest two-edged sword, cutting between soul and spirit, between joint and marrow. It exposes our innermost thoughts and desires.

—Hebrews 4:12 (NLT)

For the past several days, we've been putting on the whole *armor of God* based on Ephesians 6:11, *"Put on the whole armor of God, that you may be able to stand against the wiles of the devil."*

In Ephesians 6:17, we read that the final piece of equipment is the *sword of the Spirit*—the Word of God. When you're in a battle, your defensive strategy is important. But if a soldier only has a defense and no offense, he might hold off the enemy, but he cannot win the battle. The "sword of the Spirit" is the only piece of armor that can cut, wound, and defeat our enemy, the devil. Hebrews 4:12 describes this all-powerful tool as a *two-edged sword*, which is alive and powerful! The phrase "two-edged" comes from the Greek word *distomos*, which means "two-mouthed."

The Word of God becomes forcefully energized when it is declared by two mouths. First, the Word came out of the mouth of God. Secondly, it must come out of your mouth.

My grandkids love science experiments. One of their favorites is observing what happens when mixing baking soda and vinegar. On their own, these chemicals lie dormant, but pour vinegar on top of the baking soda, and it will begin to foam up and bubble and come alive!

Similarly, you speaking the same promises that God has already said—with confidence, backed by faith—produces life and power. It changes your environment, and it knocks out the enemy.

In the appendix to this book, you'll find "70 Promises for an Abundant Life." These promises are yours to claim. They are your inheritance as a child of God. Find the promise that fits your situation. Believe it and speak it out loud every day. Don't let the enemy get away with his plan to harm you—fight back today with the *sword of the Spirit!*

A Prayer for Today

Heavenly Father, You have fully equipped me to be a mighty man/woman of God. I put on the whole armor of God so that I win the victory and give You glory every time. I take the sword of the Spirit, the Word of God, and extinguish every fiery arrow of lies and deception the enemy throws at me. Thank You that the word always works. I stand victorious in You!

Day 92

NEVER-ALONE CHILD OF GOD

For He, Himself has said, "I will never leave you nor forsake you."

—Hebrews 13:5b

It is easy to feel overwhelmed in this chaotic and corrupt world. Do you feel like the weight of the world is on your shoulders? Are you facing a seemingly insurmountable challenge in a relationship? Are you worried about your kids? Or are you calculating how you will stretch your paycheck to the end of the month?

I want to share a powerful promise of God with you. Knowing this one promise changes everything. God Himself said, *"I will never leave you or forsake you."*

This promise is so familiar that it's easy to miss its significance. Think of this: the Creator of the universe, the One who orchestrates the rising of the sun, the One who paves His streets with gold, the One who knows you inside and out and accepts and loves you unconditionally, is beside you right now, willing and able to help you!

I challenge you to meditate on this one phrase throughout your day. God Himself said, *"I will never leave you or forsake you."* Take a moment to imagine Him with you now—holding your hand, going to that meeting with you at work, helping you minister to your wayward child, shopping for groceries, balancing the checkbook, negotiating the deal on a new house. Whatever you are doing, God is with you.

Amplified Version says it this way: *"He has said, 'I will never [under any circumstances] desert you [nor give you up nor leave you without support, nor will I in any degree leave you helpless], nor will I forsake or let you down or relax My hold on you [assuredly not]!'"*

Look at the absolutes in that promise. Father God wants to assure you that He is with you today and is willing to help you. Take God at His word. Whatever your challenge today, ask for help from the Helper who is right beside you!

A Prayer for Today

Loving Father, I am resting in this truth; You are with me today. You loved me so much that You went to the ends of the earth to save me and You're not letting go of me now. It's You and me together, always.

Day 93

SIN-FREE CHILD OF GOD

Blessed are those whose lawless deeds are forgiven, and whose sins are covered; blessed is the man to whom the Lord shall not impute sin.

—Roman 4:7–8

What separates man from God? I remember my fifth grade Sunday school teacher drawing a diagram to explain the gospel with God on one side, man on the other side and a great, uncrossable gulf between the two. She explained that sin separates man from God.

But according to our scripture for today, God is not imputing man's sins against him any longer. It says in 1 John 2:2, *"Jesus took on himself the sins of the whole world."* That is God's grace—doing for us what we could not do for ourselves.

So if Jesus took all the world's sin on Himself at the cross, then sin is no longer separating man from God. It comes down to this. The only thing keeping man from a relationship with Holy God is the answer to just one question: Will you accept Jesus as your Savior and Lord?

If you have accepted Jesus, then it says in Romans 4 that God is not counting your sins against you. God, in essence, is saying to you, *"Sin? What sin?"* God doesn't see it anymore. Because of Jesus,

God is blind to your sin. This may seem like a radical statement, but God said it.

The Living Translation says it this way, *"Oh, what joy for those whose disobedience is forgiven, whose sins are put out of sight. Yes, what joy for those whose record the Lord has cleared of sin."*

The Passion Translation says, *"What happy progress comes to them when they hear the Lord speak over them, 'I will never hold your sins against you!'"*

In I Corinthians 13:5, God's love is described as *"not irritable, and it keeps no record of being wronged."* This is great news. This means God is not mad at you for anything, He's not even in a bad mood!

I know I remind you of this often, but this is the most foundational truth necessary for enjoying an intimate relationship with your Heavenly Father. If you think God is mad at you, you'll keep your distance from Him. But He loves you and always wants you to feel welcome in His presence.

Am I saying it is okay to sin, and God doesn't care? *No.* The devil tries 24-7 to see if he can devour you by tempting you with sin. Sin opens up the door of your life to the enemy; sin has terrible consequences and will eventually make your life miserable.

I want to encourage you to keep your focus on who you are—a child of God with no sin counted against you. When you see yourself how your Father sees you, you will not hesitate to run to Him with reckless abandon to talk with your Father about everything that concerns you.

A Prayer for Today

Heavenly Father, I am so blessed, happy, and fortunate that I have been made righteous because of Jesus. Thank You that You worked out this plan to wipe out all my sins and make it possible for You and me to be best friends. I am clean. I am accepted. I am Yours!

Day 94

FEAR-CONQUERING CHILD OF GOD

For God has not given us a spirit of fear and timidity,
but of power, love, and self-discipline.

—2 Timothy 1:7

I learned a valuable lesson about fear on the Wind Walker—one I'll never forget. I had invited my sales team to my home in Colorado Springs for a weekend retreat. In the final teaching session, I gave an inspirational talk about never letting fear hold you back. I said, "Everything you want is on the other side of your comfort zone. Fear is the primary force that stands in your way of success. We can't let fear stop us."

For a team-building activity that afternoon, we went to the Cave of the Winds' Wind Walker ropes course. This course is perched precariously on top of a mountain and stands three stories high. On each level, there are cables, tiny logs, and other stepping objects suspended between poles. As you navigate the levels, each offers a more significant challenge, with the very top level hanging out over the cliff with a drop-off similar to looking down into the Grand Canyon!

We split up into two competing teams. Red and blue ribbons were tied throughout the course. The first team to capture and return all their ribbons won. I heard many groans of "You're kidding me," "I can't do that," and "No way!" Of course, the cheerleader in me enthusiastically fired up the group into action. My team chose me as their captain and said, "Wendy, you go last. You get the ribbon way out there." They said as they pointed to the red ribbon at the farthest point, on the top level on a single cable that reached out over the canyon.

Of course, we were well harnessed with safety cables and were taught how to maneuver securely through the course. As we began, there was laughter, screaming, and hollering as each team member bravely took their turn, and the others encouraged them from below.

Then it was my turn. I should tell you, I had never tried out this course before this event. I had watched my grandkids from a safe and secure spot on the ground. Looking up from the bottom, it looked like fun.

But as I climbed the first level, I felt fear rise in me that was almost paralyzing. Even writing this now, I can remember that feeling. But I had a dilemma; I was the one preaching "no fear"; this was my object lesson!

I had to negotiate with my brain to move my feet forward and push through the fear. Reaching the farthest point of the top level, I found that the path to the last red flag was across a thirty-foot rolling pole, with only a single cable above my head for balance. Looking down into the canyon and feeling the wind, I felt the fear riding on my back. But what choice did I have? I had to go forward.

With no way out, I felt myself forcefully take this tangible fear off my back and put it under my feet. I spoke to the fear and said, "Leave, in Jesus's name!" Faith and determination rose in my heart, I grabbed the flag, and our team won the race.

Fear is tangible. It is a spirit, and we can control it. In 2 Timothy 1:7, the apostle Paul told his protege, Timothy, that the "spirit of fear" does not come from God. Fear comes from the enemy, and we don't have to accept it. The devil uses fear to hold us back and stop us from the destiny God has planned for us. Fear says, "You can't trust God. He won't come through for you. You are on your own."

Faith is the opposite of fear. We are living in a scary world today. It's easy to become fearful, worried, and depressed. When you recognize fear is rising, take hold of that spirit of fear and cast it down under your feet. Let faith rise as you put your trust in God because He promises to be with you to strengthen you and help you. (Isaiah 41:10)

A Prayer for Today

Loving Father, you tell us over and over again throughout Your Word to "fear not." I realize this is for my good. You can't get all Your promises to me if I am letting fear and worry overtake me. I choose to put fear down and pick up my faith. I choose to be strong and courageous. Make me as bold as a lion!

Day 95

PRAYING AND BELIEVING CHILD OF GOD

They made war with the Hagrites, Jetur, Naphish, and Nodab.
And they were helped against them, and the Hagrites were delivered
into their hand, and all who were with them, for they cried out to
God in the battle. He heeded their prayer, because they put their
trust in Him...many fell dead, because the war was God's.

—1 Chronicles 5:20–22

I used to dismiss the Bible verses that spoke of victory over our enemies, thinking I didn't have any. Then I realized, if you are on God's side, you have enemies. One of my Bible teachers said, "If you aren't running into the devil, it's because you are both going the same direction!"

Jesus warned us in John 10:10 that the enemy's plan is to steal, kill and destroy. He constantly tries to deceive and trick people into following his plan for their destruction. Right now, he's working through legislators who are scheming to take over America and deny our freedom to worship God. Fortunately, we have a God who is greater than the most diabolic scheme the enemy can throw at us.

Today's scripture is an example of what happens when we trust in God to fight our battles. God heeded their prayer because they put their trust in Him. Their enemy was defeated because the war belonged to God!

Whether your battle today is against the takeover of our government (I hope you'll join me in prayer for this war) or an enemy takeover in your home, job, mental health, or finances—pray!

When you pray in faith, believing God to fight on your behalf, you delegate the responsibility to God. Your Almighty God and Father then assumes the obligation to win the battle. God, in essence, is saying, "It's My war now!" Your battle assignment is to continue trusting Him, listen for Holy Spirit instructions, and expect the victory.

A Prayer for Today

Dear Almighty God, my Father, it's evident that this battle is too big for me, but it's not as big as You are! I give this war over to You, Lord. Thank You that You handle this on my behalf because You love me. I will trust in You and see the victory—because the battle is Yours.

Day 96

HOLY SPIRIT-POWERED CHILD OF GOD

And being assembled together with them, He commanded them not to depart from Jerusalem, but to wait for the Promise of the Father, "which," He said, "you have heard from Me; for John truly baptized with water, but you shall be baptized with the Holy Spirit not many days from now."

—Acts 1:4–5

I grew up in a very legalistic denominational church. My Sunday school teacher taught a long list of dos and don'ts—but with no power to do the dos! Sadly, they denied the power of the Holy Spirit working in the world today. In my twenties, I gave up on trying to follow all the rules to please God and my church. It was just too hard. I decided if this is all there is to being a Christian, then no thanks. I'll just eat, drink, and be merry.

It wasn't until I was in my late thirties that I felt the Holy Spirit's sweet presence for myself and saw His power in action. I learned that the Holy Spirit is very much alive and working in churches and believers who welcome and embrace Him.

I learned about the baptism of the Holy Spirit. It's the power that I had been missing all my life! You can be saved and have your ticket to heaven, but receiving the power of the Holy Spirit into your life is when you begin to realize that salvation is *more than a ticket to heaven!*

A Christian life without the Holy Spirit's baptism is like a computer that's not plugged in. The battery runs down pretty quickly, and it becomes useless.

One of the last instructions Jesus gave His followers before He returned to heaven was to wait for the baptism of the Holy Spirit. He explained that this was a special baptism beyond water baptism. In essence, Jesus was saying, *"Don't leave home without It"*—the Holy Spirit! Don't try to minister to others, don't try to have a good marriage, don't try to be a good parent, don't try to keep yourself pure in this world, don't try to share the gospel or fulfill your purpose in your own strength—you're going to need the power of the Holy Spirit!

In the anti-Christian environment in our world today, your Heavenly Father wants to give you the power and courage you need to live a supernatural life, demonstrating God's power to those who question "Does God really exist?"

Being baptized in the Holy Spirit is essentially inviting the Holy Spirit to immerse you in Himself! It's asking Him to submerge you into His energy—to completely fill you up with Holy Spirit's supernatural, life-giving, transforming, miracle-working, dead-raising power, and world-changing boldness. It's what you were made for!

Luke 11:10, 13 says, *"For everyone who asks receives, and he who seeks finds, and to him who knocks it will be opened…how much more will your heavenly Father give the Holy Spirit to those who ask Him!"*

A Prayer for Today

Heavenly Father, I want everything You have promised to give me for a powerful, supernatural life here on earth. Please baptize me now with your Holy Spirit. By faith, I receive You. Holy Spirit, You are welcome in my life!

Day 97

POWER-TALKING CHILD OF GOD

When someone speaks in tongues, no one understands a word he says, because he's not speaking to people, but to God—he is speaking intimate mysteries in the Spirit.

—1 Corinthians 14:2 (TPT)

When I discovered the truth of this verse, it dramatically changed my view of the power and importance of speaking in tongues. Think of this; when you are speaking in the spirit, you are speaking directly to God and declaring His own plans, purposes, and kingdom agenda! God gave dominion on this earth to His children. *So when you speak out God's mysteries, you are instrumental in bringing God's will and desires to earth!*

How powerful is that?

Speaking in tongues is one of my favorite gifts—and so practical too. It is the sign that you've received the baptism of the Holy Spirit.

There are many times when I don't know how to pray for a friend or a situation, so I'll pray in English for what I think is needed, then I'll ask Holy Spirit to take over and pray through me in my special language.

Acts 2:4 reports that *"they were all filled with the Holy Spirit and began to speak with other tongues, as the Spirit gave them utterance."* God loves you so intimately that when you receive the baptism of the Holy

Spirit, He gives you your very own language between you and Him. Just as no two snowflakes are alike, no two prayer languages are alike.

I had so much false teaching about the Holy Spirit growing up—I had actually been taught that speaking in tongues was cursing God and that the Holy Spirit was not active today. So as you can imagine, I had a little trouble receiving my prayer language. Perhaps you've had a similar struggle. When I initially went to the altar, and my pastor's wife prayed for me to be baptized in the Holy Spirit, I honestly felt nothing. But I went home believing I had received and expecting to get my very own prayer language. The next day, in the shower, I was singing and praising God in English, and then little by little, new words came to me that I hadn't spoken before. I just started letting them out!

The key to receiving is desire and expectation. Mark 11:24 says, *"Therefore I say unto you, What things soever ye desire, when ye pray, believe that ye receive them, and ye shall have them."*

After you pray to receive the baptism, some syllables from your own personal God-given language will start bubbling up in your heart and come out your mouth—if you let them! As you speak by faith, you are releasing God's power and God's words out of your mouth. It's like baby talk at first, but the more you use your language, just as a baby learns to talk, you'll learn to talk to your Father in your new language too.

Don't leave this powerful gift sitting on your spiritual shelf! I encourage you to use it every day. Make it a habit to start every day by praying in your own unique language to your Heavenly Father. It connects your spirit to His Spirit and will give you more awareness of God's presence with you all day long.

A Prayer for Today

Dear Loving Father, giving me Your Holy Spirit is one more way that You have showered Your love on me. I love the fact that You and I have our own unique language, and when I speak, You know it's me. (It's like we have a secret code!) You'll be hearing from me often!

Day 98

FIRE-POWERED CHILD OF GOD

And suddenly there came a sound from heaven, as of a rushing mighty wind, and it filled the whole house where they were sitting. Then there appeared to them divided tongues, as of fire, and one sat upon each of them. And they were all filled with the Holy Spirit and began to speak with other tongues, as the Spirit gave them utterance.

—Acts 2:1–4

Can you imagine the scene?

The firepower ignited in Jesus' followers by the first baptism of the Holy Spirit at Pentecost spread the gospel across the earth. That same Holy Spirit fire continues to burn, passing on to all who have asked for it down through the church age. It is a transforming power!

Peter's transformation was astounding. Peter immediately stands before the crowd and declares the gospel of Jesus Christ with great authority! *"Men of Israel, hear these words: Jesus of Nazareth, a Man attested by God to you by miracles, wonders, and signs…you have taken by lawless hands, have crucified, and put to death; whom God raised up, having loosed the pains of death because it was not possible that He should be held by it"* (Acts 2:22–24)!

But think back a few weeks earlier—Peter was so afraid to be associated with Jesus that he lied and swore to a servant girl that he didn't even know Him.

Jesus knew that His followers could not fulfill His impossible calling on their lives without the help of Holy Spirit. The primary purpose of the baptism of the Holy Spirit is to empower each of us to boldly communicate the gospel of Jesus Christ, to confirm the Word with signs, wonders, and miracles, and to accomplish great exploits for God's kingdom here on earth.

Peter's calling was to be an evangelist, a minister of the gospel. He obviously needed the baptism of the Holy Spirit to endue him with power and boldness and strategies to preach the Word.

What are you called to do? Perhaps it's to be a mother or father. There is no function in the church more holy and sacred than parenting. Raising the next generation takes supernatural wisdom and strategies. The evangelist needs the baptism of the Holy Spirit. Pastors need it, school teachers need it, business owners need it.

Whatever God has called you to do, He planned for you to have Him as your partner. That's why He said don't leave home without the Holy Spirit's power (Acts 1:4)!

A Prayer for Today

Thank You, Jesus, that You sent us a Helper, a Comforter—the Holy Spirit—when You left earth. Holy Spirit, be my tour guide! Teach me to be aware of Your presence and to listen for Your voice to lead me today so that I can accomplish all that You've destined me to do.

Day 99

Triumphant Child of God

Having disarmed principalities and powers, He made a
public spectacle of them, triumphing over them in it.

—Colossians 2:15

In the late 1980s, Frank Peretti wrote a book, *This Present Darkness*. The fictional story is set in the small town of Ashton. When a skeptical reporter and a prayerful, hardworking minister began to investigate mysterious happenings, they suddenly found themselves caught up in a sinister New Age plot to enslave the townspeople and eventually the entire human race. The physical world meets the spiritual realm as war raged between forces of good and evil.

When the book was released, a well-known leader in the Christian community adamantly warned us not to read the book or have anything to do with the devil because "he was much more powerful than we are."

Unfortunately, that is the belief of many Christians, which is why the devil is getting away with wreaking havoc in our world today. But according to Colossians 2:15, Jesus stripped the devil and demons of every bit of power, overcame them all, rose again, took back the keys to death and hades, and gave authority on earth back to His children!

The Greek word translated "triumphing over" in Colossians 2:15 means "to make an acclamatory procession." This is specifically referring to the Romans' "triumphant procession" after defeating their enemies.

Upon conquering an enemy, the Romans would hold a parade. They would take the dethroned king, strip him, and drag him through the crowd behind the conquering king for all their subjects to see. He would be humiliated and insulted, but that's not all. They would also cut off the thumbs of his hands and the big toes of both feet. This was to assure the citizens of the kingdom that this enemy would never be a threat to any of them again. There was no need to fear him anymore. Any rumor about him ever challenging Rome again would be scoffed at because the citizens had seen him in the parade.[†]

The same thing happened to the devil. Jesus didn't just defeat the devil, escape hell, and overcome death. He had a triumphant procession to display the devil to the universe as a totally conquered foe! That's what this verse is referring to.

As a child of God, you have been deputized and authorized to enforce the victory Jesus won over the enemy: remind the devil of the parade demonstrating his defeat! I like what Andrew Wommack said, "If you need to speak to the devil, talk to the bottom of your shoe because he's under your feet!"

The only thing the devil has left is a big mouth, and he uses it to lie and deceive and throw doubts, causing you to question your identity and become fearful. Fear gives power to the enemy. So stand your ground. Kick the devil out of your family, finances, home, and all that concerns you. Don't be the victim; take your place as the victor!

A Prayer for Today

Lord, thank you for defeating the enemy on my behalf. You are my Hero, my Champion! You have won the victory and stripped the enemy of his power to destroy me. So I declare that I am victorious in You. No scheme of the enemy will overtake me. I stand my ground and enforce the victory that is already mine.

[†] Note from Andrew Wommack, *Spiritual Authority*.

Day 100

Confidently Violent Child of God

*When the seventy missionaries returned to Jesus, they were
ecstatic with joy, telling him, "Lord, even the demons
obeyed us when we commanded them in your name!"*

—Luke 10:17 (TPT)

The Bible makes it clear that as a child of God operating in the power of Jesus Christ, you have authority over the devil and demon forces. Avery took this truth seriously.

I met Avery while working in the children's program at Andrew Wommack's Summer Family Bible Conference. Avery was ten years old and a participant in my small group. We discussed how important it is to cast all our cares on the Lord because He lovingly cares for us. Avery spoke up and told our group, "It is impossible for me not to worry because I was diagnosed with severe anxiety." Several times throughout the week, she became extremely fearful, sweating, and shaking uncontrollably.

While praying for Avery, the Lord showed me that this anxiety was the enemy trying (and so far, succeeding) in stealing her peace.

The Holy Spirit gave me an illustration to help her understand how to fight and not give in to the enemy's scheme.

I asked Avery, "What is your favorite thing in your whole house?"

Without hesitation, she answered, "My dachshund."

I asked, "So, Avery, if a robber came into your house and tried to take your dog, what would you do? What would you say?"

She didn't hesitate for a moment. She stood up and boldly announced with fire in her voice, "*There'd be violence!*"

It was the perfect answer.

I told her that just like a robber trying to steal her dachshund, the devil is trying to steal her peace. She needed to respond in the same way. With confident violence! James 4:7 (TPT) says, *"So then, surrender to God. Stand up to the devil and resist him, and he will turn and run away from you."*

I told her not to beg God to take away the anxiety; God already gave her the authority over the devil. Speak to the anxiety; tell it to leave. Command the devil to take his hands off you, in the name of Jesus!

The Word promises that the devil has to obey you. He can be stubborn and sometimes doesn't go away quickly, but keep resisting him, and he must turn and run.

Is there a robber in your house today? Is the devil trying to steal something from your life? Your peace? Your joy? Your health? Use your authority and confident violence! Make him turn tail and run. You have the authority in Jesus' name!

A Prayer for Today

Heavenly Father, now I see it. I've been allowing the enemy to run all over me. But I am not letting him anymore. Jesus came so that I can have an abundant life, and I am grabbing hold of it in every area of my life. I'm kicking the devil out the door! Thank You for the authority to use Jesus' name.

Day 101

Life Beyond Your Wildest Dreams

And I pray that He would unveil within you the unlimited riches of His glory and favor until supernatural strength floods your innermost being with His divine might and explosive power. Then, by constantly using your faith, the life of Christ will be released deep inside you, and the resting place of his love will become the very source and root of your life. Then you will be empowered to discover what every holy one experiences—the great magnitude of the astonishing love of Christ in all its dimensions. How deeply intimate and far-reaching is his love! How enduring and inclusive it is! Endless love beyond measurement that transcends our understanding—this extravagant love pours into you until you are filled to overflowing with the fullness of God! Never doubt God's mighty power to work in you and accomplish all this. He will achieve infinitely more than your greatest request, your most unbelievable dream, and exceed your wildest imagination! He will outdo them all, for his miraculous power constantly energizes you.

—Ephesians 3:16–20 (TPT)

As we come to the last day of this book, I hope you're beginning to realize that trusting Jesus Christ as your Savior gives you a lot *more than a ticket to heaven!*

I want to leave you with a prayer that when believed and received, will have consequences beyond your wildest dreams! The apostle Paul prayed this prayer for the disciples entrusted to his ministry. I am so thankful that he recorded it for all of us to pray.

As I was meditating on this prayer, I noticed that there is only one request in this prayer; it's made in verse 16. The four following verses explain the benefits received through the granting of the prayer request in verse 16.

Here's the request: *"that the Father would unveil within you the unlimited riches of His glory and favor."*

The word *glory* in Greek means *"true reality, view, and opinion."* In other words, the "riches of His glory" is the understanding of the reality of God, His unending love and favor toward you, and to understand His view and opinion of you.

True reality is not what religion has taught you about God. And it's not what you think of yourself but what God says is true of you and what the Bible says is true about God.

The benefits promised from this revelation are mind-boggling—supernatural strength, divine might, explosive power, experiencing His endless love beyond measure! Ultimately, it is the life of Christ released in you.

I challenge you to pray this prayer every day. See how God reveals Himself to you and gives you a revelation of His view and opinion of you. Matthew 7:7 promises that when you ask, you shall receive.

A Prayer for Today

Heavenly Father, I am asking You, just like the apostle Paul did, that You would unveil within me the unlimited riches of Your glory and favor. I choose to walk daily in the revelation of my righteous identity, receiving all the inheritance that Jesus bought for me at the cross, and I pray that I will live my life influencing others to come to a loving understanding of Your grace and love, in Jesus' name. Amen!

Appendix

70 Promises for an Abundant Life

I Am Accepted and Made Righteous

Jesus made me righteous. (2 Corinthians 5:21) "For He made Him who knew no sin to be sin for us, that we might become the righteousness of God in Him."

I reign in life through Jesus Christ. (Romans 5:17) "For if by the one man's offense death reigned through the one, much more those who receive abundance of grace and of the gift of righteousness will reign in life through the One, Jesus Christ."

I believe God, and so I am made righteous. (Genesis 15:6) "And Abraham believed God, and He accounted it to him for righteousness."

I can know God personally. (Philippians 3:8–10) "That I may gain Christ and be found in Him, not having my own righteousness, which is from the law, but that which is through faith in Christ, the righteousness which is from God by faith; that I may know Him and the power of His resurrection."

My faith credits me with righteousness. (Romans 4:5–6) "But to him who does not work but believes on Him who justifies the ungodly, his faith is accounted for righteousness, just as David also describes the blessedness of the man to whom God imputes righteousness apart from works."

I am an heir to the promises with Abraham. (Romans 4:13) "For the promise that he would be the heir of the world was not to

Abraham or to his seed through the law, but through the righteousness of faith."

Grace reigns in my life. (Romans 5:21) "So that as sin reigned in death, even so grace might reign through righteousness to eternal life through Jesus Christ our Lord."

I am on the path of life. (Proverbs 12:28) "In the way of righteousness is life, and in its pathway there is no death."

I am accepted by God. It's a free gift I can't earn. (Ephesians 2:8–9) "For by grace you have been saved through faith, and that not of yourselves; it is the gift of God, not of works, lest anyone should boast."

Good things come to me because I've been made righteous. (Proverbs 13:21–22) "Evil pursues sinners, but to the righteous, good shall be repaid. A good man leaves an inheritance to his children's children, but the wealth of the sinner is stored up for the righteous."

I Am Fearless

I am rescued from evil. (Galatians 1:3-4) Grace to you and peace from God the Father and our Lord Jesus Christ, who gave Himself for our sins, that He might deliver us from this present evil age, according to the will of our God and Father.

I will not fear when God is my helper, (Hebrews 13:6) "So we can confidently say, 'The Lord is my helper; I will not fear; what can man do to me?'"

I trust in God alone. (Proverbs 29:25) "The fear of man brings a snare, but whoever trusts in the Lord shall be safe."

I am strong and courageous. (1 Chronicles 28:20) "I will not be afraid or discouraged, for the Lord, my God, is with me. He will not fail me or forsake me."

I have been deputized with dominion on earth. (Genesis 1:28) "Then God blessed them, and God said to them, 'Be fruitful and multiply; fill the earth and subdue it; have dominion over the fish of the sea, over the birds of the air, and over every living thing that moves on the earth.'"

I am above my problems, not beneath them. (Deuteronomy 28:13) "And the Lord will make you the head and not the tail; you shall be above only, and not be beneath, if you heed the commandments of the Lord your God, which I command you today, and are careful to observe *them.*"

I am redeemed from the enemy. (Psalm 107:2) "Let the redeemed of the Lord say so, Whom He has redeemed from the hand of the enemy."

I belong to God. (Isaiah 43:1) "But now, thus says the Lord, who created you, O Jacob, And He who formed you, O Israel: 'Fear not, for I have redeemed you; I have called you by your name; You are Mine.'"

I am loved. (John 3:16) "For God so loved the world that He gave His only begotten Son, that whoever believes in Him should not perish but have everlasting life."

I am never out of His sight. (Isaiah 49:16) "See, I have inscribed you on the palms of My hands; Your walls are continually before Me."

I am more than a conqueror. (Romans 8:37) "Yet in all these things we are more than conquerors through Him who loved us."

I Am Forgiven and Guilt Free

He forgives all my sins. (Psalm 103:2–4) "Bless the LORD, O my soul, and forget not all His benefits: Who forgives all my iniquities, Who heals all my diseases, Who redeems my life from destruction, Who crowns me with lovingkindness and tender mercies."

God is not mad at me. (John 3:17) "For God did not send His Son into the world to condemn the world, but that the world through Him might be saved."

Jesus is my Savior. (Acts 5:30–31) "The God of our fathers raised up Jesus whom you murdered by hanging on a tree. God has exalted Him to His right hand *to be* Prince and Savior, to give repentance to Israel and forgiveness and release from sins."

I am forgiven. (1 John 1:9) "If we confess our sins, He is faithful and just to forgive us our sins and to cleanse us from all unrighteousness."

I am a new creation. (2 Corinthians 5:17) "Therefore, if anyone is in Christ, he is a new creation; old things have passed away; behold, all things have become new."

I am completely redeemed. (Colossians 1:13–14) "For he has rescued us from the dominion of darkness and brought us into the kingdom of the Son he loves, in whom we have redemption, the forgiveness of sins."

All my sin was nailed to Jesus' cross. (Colossians 2:14 NLT) "Then God made you alive with Christ, for he forgave all our sins. He canceled the record of the charges against us and took it away by nailing it to the cross."

I have a covenant with God for my forgiveness. (Matthew 26:28, *Jesus speaking*) "This is my blood of the covenant, which is poured out for many for the forgiveness of sins."

God does not remember my sin. (Hebrews 8:12 NLT) "For I will forgive their wickedness and will remember their sins no more."

Grace forgives all sin. (Ephesians 1:7) "In him we have redemption through his blood, the forgiveness of sins, in accordance with the riches of God's grace."

Love covers sin. (1 Peter 4:8) Above all things have fervent love for one another, for "love covers over a multitude of sins."

I Am Prosperous

When I seek first God's kingdom I will have all I need. (Matthew 6:33) "But seek first the kingdom of God and His righteousness, and all these things shall be added to you."

I demonstrate that God is my Provider by giving my tithe. (Malachi 3:10) "'Bring all the tithes into the storehouse, that there may be food in My house, and try Me now in this,' says the Lord of hosts. 'If I will not open for you the windows of heaven and pour out for you *such* blessing that there will not be room enough to receive it.'"

God's grace makes me rich. (2 Corinthians 8:9) "For you know the grace of our Lord Jesus Christ, that though He was rich, yet for your sakes He became poor, that you through His poverty might become rich."

I have power to get wealth. (Deuteronomy 8:18) "And you shall remember the Lord your God, for it is He who gives you power to get wealth, that He may establish His covenant which He swore to your fathers, as it is this day."

God commands blessing on me. (Deuteronomy 28:8) "The Lord will command the blessing on you in your storehouses and in all to which you set your hand, and He will bless you in the land which the Lord your God is giving you."

The curses are broken, I only get the blessings. (Galatians 3:13–14) "Christ has redeemed us from the curse of the law, having become a curse for us (for it is written, 'Cursed is everyone who hangs on a tree'), that the blessing of Abraham might come upon the Gentiles in Christ Jesus, that we might receive the promise of the Spirit through faith."

I am an heir to the promised blessing. (Galatians 3:29) "And if you are Christ's, then you are Abraham's seed, and heirs according to the promise."

God is my provider. (Philippians 4:19) "And my God shall supply all your need according to His riches in glory by Christ Jesus."

I sow seed with my giving, expecting a harvest. (Proverbs 3:9–10) "Honor the Lord with your possessions, and with the first-fruits of all your increase; so your barns will be filled with plenty, and your vats will overflow with new wine."

God gives me money for giving and living. (2 Corinthians 9:10–11) "Now may He who supplies seed to the sower, and bread for food, supply and multiply the seed you have sown and increase the fruits of your righteousness, while you are enriched in everything for all liberality, which causes thanksgiving through us to God."

My Father is generous and holds nothing back from me. (Romans 8:32) "He who did not spare His own Son, but delivered Him up for us all, how shall He not with Him also freely give us all things?"

I Am Healed

Jesus took a terrible beating for me to be healed. (Isaiah 53:4–5) "Surely He has borne our griefs and carried our sorrows; yet we esteemed Him stricken, smitten by God, and afflicted. But He was wounded for our transgressions, He was bruised for our iniquities; the chastisement for our peace was upon Him, and by His stripes we are healed."

Jesus lives in me. What is true of Jesus, is true of me. (Romans 8:11) "But if the Spirit of Him who raised Jesus from the dead dwells in you, He who raised Christ from the dead will also give life to your mortal bodies through His Spirit who dwells in you."

I believe my healing will manifest. (Isaiah 58:8) "Then your light shall break forth like the morning, your healing shall spring forth speedily, and your righteousness shall go before you; the glory of the Lord shall be your rear guard."

I speak the word, and I am healed. (Psalm 107:19–20) "Then they cried out to the Lord in their trouble, and He saved them out of their distresses. He sent His word and healed them, and delivered them from their destructions."

I agree with God's Word. What I speak I create. (Psalm 118:17) "I shall not die, but live, and declare the works of the Lord."

I am blessed. Healing is part of the blessing. (Deuteronomy 7:15) "And the Lord will take away from you all sickness, and will afflict you with none of the terrible diseases of Egypt which you have known, but will lay them on all those who hate you."

Jesus paid dearly for my healing at the cross. (1 Peter 2:24) "Who Himself bore our sins in His own body on the tree, that we, having died to sins, might live for righteousness—by whose stripes you were healed."

Healing is God's plan for me. (Mark 16:17–18) "And these signs will follow those who believe: In My name they will cast out demons; they will speak with new tongues; they will take up serpents; and if they drink anything deadly, it will by no means hurt them; they will lay hands on the sick, and they will recover."

God wants me well. (Matthew 8:2–3) "And behold, a leper came and worshipped Him, saying, 'Lord, if You are willing, You can make me clean.' Then Jesus put out His hand and touched him, saying, 'I am willing; be cleansed.' Immediately his leprosy was cleansed."

Healing is part of salvation. (Psalm 103:2–3) "Bless the Lord, O my soul, and forget not all His benefits: Who forgives all your iniquities, who heals all your diseases."

I HAVE FAVOR

I am engulfed with favor. (Psalm 5:12) "For You, O Lord, will bless the righteous; with favor You will surround him as with a shield."

I can always expect abundance and mercy. (Psalm 23:5–6) "You prepare a table before me in the presence of my enemies; You anoint my head with oil; my cup runs over. Surely goodness and mercy shall follow me all the days of my life; and I will dwell in the house of the Lord forever."

God is gracious to me. I have peace. (Numbers 6:25–26) "The Lord make His face shine upon you, and be gracious to you; the Lord lift up His countenance upon you, and give you peace."

God's favor on me is obvious to others. (Genesis 39:3–4) "And his master saw that the Lord was with him and that the Lord made all he did to prosper in his hand. So Joseph found favor in his sight."

God cares for me. He loves me. (Job 10:12) "You have granted me life and favor, and Your care has preserved my spirit."

I was created to dominate and overcome. (Psalm 8:4–6) "What is man that You are mindful of him, and the son of man that You visit him? For You have made him a little lower than Elohim, and You have crowned him with glory and honor. You have made him to have dominion over the works of Your hands; You have put all things under his feet."

I seek God, and He rewards me. (Hebrews 11:6) "And without faith it is impossible to please him, for whoever would draw near to

God must believe that he exists and that he rewards those who seek him."

I am redeemed and energized with good things. (Psalm 103:4–5) "Who redeems your life from destruction, who crowns you with lovingkindness and tender mercies, who satisfies your mouth with good things, so that your youth is renewed like the eagle's."

I am confident of God's mercy and grace when I need it most. (Hebrews 4:16) "Let us therefore come boldly to the throne of grace, that we may obtain mercy and find grace to help in time of need."

I am Influential

I carry the gospel message everywhere I go. (1 Peter 2:9) "But you are a chosen race, a royal priesthood, a holy nation, a people for his own possession, that you may proclaim the excellences of him who called you out of darkness into his marvelous light."

I influence others with right living. (Proverbs 12:26) "One who is righteous is a guide to his neighbor, but the way of the wicked leads them astray."

I boldly stand up for righteousness. (1 Peter 2:12) "Keep your conduct among the Gentiles honorable, so that when they speak against you as evildoers, they may see your good deeds and glorify God on the day of visitation."

God's grace gives me the right words at the right time. (1 Peter 3:15) "But in your hearts honor Christ the Lord as holy, always being prepared to make a defense to anyone who asks you for a reason for the hope that is in you; yet do it with gentleness and respect."

My lifestyle sets a godly example for others. (1 Timothy 4:12) "Let no one despise you for your youth, but set the believers an example in speech, in conduct, in love, in faith, in purity."

God gives me wisdom for every situation. (Daniel 12:3) "And those who are wise shall shine like the brightness of the sky above; and those who turn many to righteousness, like the stars forever and ever."

I have victory over the devil and demon activity. (1 John 4:4) "You are of God, little children, and have overcome them, because He who is in you is greater than he who is in the world."

I am righteous and wise and love to learn. (Proverbs 9:9) "Give instruction to a wise man, and he will be still wiser; teach a righteous man, and he will increase in learning."

I boldly stand for what is good. (Romans 12:21) "Do not be overcome by evil, but overcome evil with good."

I am a king and priest in God's kingdom. (Revelation 1:5b-6) "To Him who loved us and washed us from our sins in His own blood, and has made us kings and priests to His God and Father, to Him be glory and dominion forever and ever. Amen."

About the Author

Wendy Lee Kremer is a graduate of Charis Bible College in Woodland Park, Colorado, with graduate studies in World Outreach. She is a licensed minister of the gospel of Jesus Christ, an international conference speaker, Bible teacher, author, Christian blogger, and daily disciple of Jesus. She is passionate about dispelling legalistic religious teachings, ministering God's love and grace, and cultivating intimacy with God free from condemnation and guilt.

By applying God's promises and the principles she teaches in this book, she and her husband Don have developed several businesses, including a trucking company and an award-winning online nutrition business. They have also helped many other entrepreneurs establish successful businesses.

Wendy and Don have been married thirty-four years and are blessed with four children, ten grandchildren, and a growing number of great-grandchildren. Having lived in the Midwest most of their lives, they now enjoy the snow-free winters of Arizona, serving at Vida Church in Mesa.